"Wrought from the trenches of actual leadership stories and immersed in biblical teaching, *Broken and Whole* gently pries itself into the gritty places of the soul and invites God to meet us. . . . Steve Macchia's consistent candor and authenticity coupled with gentle guidance—and his killer questions!—will take you there. Steve's final words express the best gift this book can offer—a path by which to live, love and lead in the name of God: Father, Son and Holy Spirit. Amen."

Mindy Caliguire, founder and president, Soul Care,
author of *STIR: Spiritual Transformation in Relationships*

"Steve Macchia has been nosing around our churches and ministries—especially our board meetings. But the good news: instead of meddling, he ministers. When you read chapter four, 'The Tight Grip of Pride and Close-Fisted Greed,' you'll discover a new standard of leader and author transparency. Steve bares it all—and his authenticity ensured I would read every chapter: slowly, prayerfully, confessionally. Every Christian leader—every Christ-follower—will relate to the powerful stories that launch each chapter and the probing Spiritual Leadership Audit questions that conclude each chapter. *Broken and Whole* is a must-read."

John Pearson, author of *Mastering the Management Buckets*

"I love this book! It's honest, hopeful and biblically grounded. In *Broken and Whole* Steve Macchia invites us to explore a number of common habits and patterns that so often go unchecked and yet have grave consequences for our interactions with others. In these pages we find a helpful paradox: facing our brokenness clears space for God to bring something really special—authentic transformation."

Nathan Foster, Andrews Chair of Spiritual Formation, Spring Arbor University,
author of *The Making of an Ordinary Saint*

"Being healed from the inside out by the love of God is a necessary and ongoing process for every believer living in our broken world, and even more critical for Christian leaders. *Broken and Whole* is a wonderful tool for leaders to utilize in this journey toward wholeness. Read it, reflect, and no doubt, God will use it to do a deep work in your life."

Jane Overstreet, president and CEO, Development Associates International

"I once heard a greatly respected spiritual formation writer muse, 'Wouldn't it be good if people would talk about their weaknesses as a way of introducing themselves.' And this is exactly the pattern of transparency Steve Macchia follows as he talks about his own brokenness before describing his path to change. What a wonderful way to present the wholeness described in 1 Corinthians 13—the love that is God's, the love that can bubble up within the leader."

Gary W. Moon, Dallas Willard Center, Westmont College,
editor of *Eternal Living*

"*Broken and Whole* is not just another book about authentic Christian leadership. Through Steve's transparency of his brokenness we gain extraordinary insights into how patience and kindness may be restored in our lives. He challenges us to embrace our brokenness and unlock the keys for leading boldly in a day of great challenges. As I read *Broken and Whole*, over and over I heard the Holy Spirit speaking directly to me. I am confident the same will be true for you when you read this outstanding book."

Dan Busby, president, ECFA

"I've just finished reading my friend Steve Macchia's new book, *Broken and Whole*. It combines Steve's long experience with leaders and organizations, wise practices, Scripture, and very practical applications for every leader. Don't miss the chapter on rudeness, a neglected teaching in many contexts. And pay attention to all the end of chapter application areas—this is where you will grow the most and redeem the investment in this new work."

Dave Travis, Chief Executive and Encouragement Officer, Leadership Network

"I have known Steve Macchia for more than thirty years and I can assure you that Steve has consistently and passionately loved Jesus and the church all these years. I know of no one more qualified to gently guide the reader into a deeper understanding of the relationship between brokenness and the generous love of Jesus. . . . Theologically rich and practically informed, *Broken and Whole* will challenge you to abandon a shallow understanding of brokenness and instead discover the joy of wholeness, only discovered at the feet of Jesus. I highly recommend this book for anyone seeking a deeper, fuller, richer understanding of the love of Jesus in the midst of a broken world."

Jimmy Dodd, PastorServe, author of *Survive or Thrive*

"The greatest commandment for leaders isn't any different than the greatest commandment for anyone. Love God. Love people. Stephen has given us a vision of Christian leadership that is more patient than hurried, more Jesus-promoting than self-promoting and more generous than self-serving. His candor and humble self-revelation is inviting and grace-giving. I highly recommend *Broken and Whole*."

Alan Fadling, executive director, The Leadership Institute, author of *An Unhurried Life*

BROKEN
AND
WHOLE

A Leader's Path to
Spiritual Transformation

Stephen A. Macchia

An imprint of InterVarsity Press
Downers Grove, Illinois

InterVarsity Press
P.O. Box 1400, Downers Grove, IL 60515-1426
ivpress.com
email@ivpress.com

*InterVarsity Press® is the book-publishing division of InterVarsity Christian Fellowship/USA®, a
movement of students and faculty active on campus at hundreds of universities, colleges and schools
of nursing in the United States of America, and a member movement of the International Fellowship
of Evangelical Students. For information about local and regional activities, visit intervarsity.org.*

*All Scripture quotations, unless otherwise indicated, are taken from the Holy Bible, New
International Version®. NIV®. Copyright ©1973, 1978, 1984 by International Bible Society. Used by
permission of Zondervan Publishing House. All rights reserved.*

*Some names and identifying information in this book's stories have been changed to protect the
privacy of individuals. The details of some stories are composites of actual people and events.*

Cover design: Cindy Kiple
Interior design: Beth McGill
Images: © Kritchanut/iStockphoto

ISBN 978-0-8308-4606-1 (print)
ISBN 978-0-8308-9917-3 (digital)

Printed in the United States of America ∞

Library of Congress Cataloging-in-Publication Data

Names: Macchia, Stephen A., 1956-
Title: Broken and whole : a leader's path to spiritual transformation /
    Stephen A. Macchia.
Description: Downers Grove : InterVarsity Press, 2015. | Includes
    bibliographical references.
Identifiers: LCCN 2015036013 | ISBN 9780830846061 (pbk. : alk. paper)
Classification: LCC BS2675.52 .M23 2015 | DDC 253--dc23
LC record available at http://lccn.loc.gov/2015036013

P 20 19 18 17 16 15 14 13 12 11 10 9 8 7 6 5 4 3 2 1
Y 32 31 30 29 28 27 26 25 24 23 22 21 20 19 18 17 16 15

This book is dedicated to the suffering, heartache, sinfulness and imperfections of my life, all of which are teaching me to trust and love God with my whole heart, soul, mind and strength.

Only through the ongoing restoration of God's steadfast love within my soul can I offer redemptive and transformative love to my neighbor as myself.

May it be so in my heart and yours, graciously and gratefully for the glory of God:

Father, Son and Holy Spirit.

Amen.

The LORD is the everlasting God,
the Creator of the ends of the earth.
He will not grow tired or weary,
and his understanding no one can fathom.
He gives strength to the weary
and increases the power of the weak.
Even youths grow tired and weary,
and young men stumble and fall;
but those who hope in the LORD
will renew their strength.
They will soar on wings like eagles;
they will run and not grow weary,
they will walk and not be faint.

ISAIAH 40:28-31

For we are God's handiwork, [re]created in
Christ Jesus to do good works, which God
prepared in advance for us to do.

EPHESIANS 2:10 (NIV)

Contents

Behold the patient love of God
Become what you receive
Behold the kind love of God
Become what you receive
Behold the protecting love of God
Become what you receive
Behold the trusting love of God
Become what you receive
Behold the hopeful love of God
Become what you receive
Behold the persevering love of God
Become what you receive
Behold the unconditional love of God
It does not envy, it does not boast
It is not proud, it is not rude
It is not self-seeking, it is not easily angered
It keeps no record of wrongs,
it does not delight in evil but rejoices in the truth
It never fails
Prophecies, tongues and knowledge will cease,
still and pass away
Faith, hope and love remain
But the greatest of these is love
Become what you receive

1 Corinthians 13: 4-13
as adapted by Stephen Macchia

Introduction

An Invitation to Discover Strength in Weakness

The most excellent way

THE MOST DYNAMIC SPIRITUAL LEADERS know they are both saint and sinner. Or, as Martin Luther noted long ago, *"Simul iustus et peccator"*—at the same time righteous and sinner. These leaders live with a burning desire to be honest about themselves—acknowledging their strengths as well as their struggles and mishaps. They live and lead from the depth of their soul, which is the essence of their existence. And, as a result, they become more attuned to an experiential knowledge of the truth about God and others within their reach.

Healthy spiritual leaders recognize the reality of living in the tension of the already-and-not-yet nature of the kingdom. They expect to experience both transformative redemption *and* continued brokenness in their generational lifetime. They know that Christ's kingdom has been inaugurated and is being realized here on earth. But their complete redemption is not fully consummated until they are ushered into God's kingdom for all eternity.

As continuously redeemed and transformed beings, they experience the abundant life of Christ with ever-increasing joy and thereby invite others around them to do likewise. Leaders who embrace their brokenness and submit it authentically into the hands of God are the ones who marvel at God's redemptive work and serve others with renewed passion. Their spiritual eyesight is likened to Saint Augustine, who once said, "In my deepest wound I saw your glory, and it dazzled me." They are an inspiration to all.

Consider this perspective on leadership as portrayed in the biblical text. For example, where would the story of Joseph's tested faithfulness be without the jealousy of his brothers or the lure from Potiphar's wife? Would we know about the leader Moses without his excuse of a speech impediment and shirking responsibilities? And—oh by the way—what about his murder of an Egyptian? Wasn't Rahab the harlot an instrument of grace for Joshua? What about Saul's blatant hatred of Christians before being blinded by the light on the road to Damascus? And would we know the full gospel story without Jesus suffering from ridicule, beatings, humiliation and the excruciating pain of a broken body and shed blood on the cross?

I am profoundly motivated when I think of the woman who was abused by her mother growing up and who now serves as a mentor to young moms. I'm deeply touched by the severely disabled woman who is a faithful servant leader, stuffing envelopes and fervently praying for missionaries in the agency where she volunteers time and resources. I'm awestruck by the former drug addict and ex-con who now is clean and sober and leading troubled youth to Christ. I'm moved by the fallen leader who, once caught in a web of lies and an adulterous relationship, is back with his wife and together serving couples in marital difficulty. I'm equally delighted when I meet many other leaders who are simply willing to own their brokenness, no matter how messy or complex, and who humbly submit that weakness into the hands of Almighty God to become a redeemed strength unlike any of their natural abilities.

BLESSED AND BROKEN

I'm dearly loved by my heavenly Father and I'm deeply sinful—how can the two go together?

I've been a leader myself for nearly four decades. I've had the privilege of serving others in local church, parachurch and nonprofit environments. I've experienced great success and a few embarrassing failures. I've seen incredible highs and a handful of deep lows. I've considered myself effective and I've watched myself tire into utter exhaustion. I've brought others a lot of joy and I've both dished out and received from others my share of disappointment. In essence, as much as I like to view myself as a good or even a very good leader, I'm more truthfully a blessed and broken leader, one who is daily in need of being restored and renewed, refreshed and redeemed by the Spirit of God who resides in me.

Basically, I've come to grips with the reality that I am who I am. I'm a new creation in Christ Jesus. I have made many positive contributions as a leader. I've served faithfully as a pastor in a large and healthy church. I've experienced effectiveness as a leader of a one-hundred-year-old organization that grew significantly in my tenure. I've mentored many young and aspiring leaders. I've even founded a ministry that's been richly blessed by God.

But I also make mistakes. I blunder. I think horrible thoughts. I'm an internal quagmire more often than I desire and in continual need of God's grace. I know what it feels like to be a manipulator, and when not kept in check I can drive myself and others crazy with my perfectionistic tendencies. I've been deeply hurt by past failures. I've been disappointed by the attitudes and actions of others. And I see these same things in many others who are in leadership positions in the body of Christ.

I've discovered that when I'm authentic, honest and transparent about *all* my realities as a leader, I can relax more in the presence of those who previously intimidated me. I can laugh more at my own imperfections. I can live in a deep place of freedom and joy. Most importantly, I can embrace my brokenness, befriend it, and watch and wait in trust for God to birth hope in my heart for the redemptive way forward. In essence, by living in this reality I can experience the fullness of a loving God and the richness of an emancipated consciousness that leads me into genuine freedom and joy.

I'm willing to embrace my own blessed and broken reality. I know that my Almighty God sees me as his dearly loved, graced and gifted child, and he sees me at my worst when I'm a disheartened follower or a disobedient sinner. And he loves me no matter what state I'm in. I can trust his Spirit to redeem the reality of my brokenness, and I can live in the hope of the resurrection, willing to die to myself, live fully for God, and offer myself as a living sacrifice to all who cross my path in life and service. There's no better way to live and lead.

WELCOME TO THE JOURNEY

So I ask you: What's your choice as a leader today? Will you confess your own belovedness and blessedness as well as your brokenness?

If so, I invite you to join me in entering into the truth about the abundant life we have as dearly loved and richly blessed Christ-followers and to embrace our brokenness as human beings in constant need of God's grace. For the sake of this book, and with no intention to standardize these categories, I'm using *brokenness* or *weakness* as overarching terms. Underneath those terms are four subsets to note, representing both internal brokenness (our own sinful choices and painful misfortunes) and external brokenness (the effect of others' sin on us and the impact of our world's large calamities):

1. Suffering—physical disabilities, emotional illness, societal misfortune, catastrophic events, inflicted without your individual or human choice

2. Heartache—physical or emotional abuse, disappointments in others or in life circumstances (mistakes, struggles, mishaps and shortcomings), shame and guilt, or relational discord afflicted by others and/or contributed also by you

3. Sinfulness—prideful choices you've made that create internal or external pain for yourself and/or others and that reflect outright disobedience to God, regardless of motivation or rationale

4. Imperfections—those areas of your life that seem to follow you daily, such as your idiosyncratic behaviors, nagging habits and plaguing mind games that keep you up at night

I will lead the way by telling you the truth about me. I'm willing to do this because I'm concerned about the growing need for authentic Christian leadership today. And, I'm alarmed at how many are allergic to doing the hard work of looking deep within to discover their true selves and upward to God for his unique blessing on their lives. Instead, many leaders are living unfulfilled lives without really knowing why. Some are simply unwilling to confess their brokenness or acknowledge their weakness. Others are looking for the perfect leader somewhere "out there" to emulate.

Many want to follow leaders who appear put together; we want to be tutored by them in order to look and sound like them. We will do whatever it takes to reach their perceived status and recognition. We read their books, attend their conferences, practice their programs, buy their products and begin to speak like them (sometimes even exploiting their published sermons and teaching outlines). We want to somehow acquire their strength without considering the cost they too have paid (and the suffering they endured) in addressing their own brokenness and seeing how God has redeemed it and continues to redeem it for his glory.

We long to have what others have earned. We dream about our walls being filled with the same framed accolades these emulated leaders have achieved. We measure ourselves against the success of others. Yet the upward ascent to greatness feels more like pushing a rock uphill, and we are forced to work all the harder so we aren't found out as a failure, a fraud or a quitter.

I'm convinced that the true pursuit of greatness as a leader begins and continues in the gentle humility that accompanies our sincere confession of brokenness and the accompanying need for God to heal, redeem and strengthen us from the inside out. My simple invitation in this book is for you to confess your brokenness in the context of your belovedness and your blessedness—not just once but on an ongoing basis—and then to lead others as you have been led by God: in love.

By giving voice and words to your brokenness, you can indeed experience the depth of soul and vitality of service you've longed for, though it will most likely look much different from what you could ever ask, dream or imagine today. Strength will emerge out of weakness—if you prayerfully submit all of yourself in trust to God. Best of all: the true you will emerge like never before, as you become all that God intends.

Therefore, let's remember with gratefulness Paul's paradoxical insights in 2 Corinthians 12:9-10:

> "My grace is sufficient for you, for my power is made perfect in weakness." Therefore I will boast all the more gladly about my weaknesses, so that Christ's power may rest on me. That is why, for Christ's sake, I delight in weaknesses, in insults, in hardships, in persecutions, in difficulties. For when I am weak, then I am strong.

God delights to welcome you with his loving embrace into a countercultural way of leading and following—from a broken and redeemed heart overflowing with humility, grace and love. Then and only then will you be made whole.

THE MOST EXCELLENT WAY

In the book of 1 Corinthians, the apostle Paul writes lovingly and directly to a troubled and broken church and invites its leaders to allow God's love to heal, redeem and transform them from the inside out. Paul speaks very specifically into their brokenness: divisions in the church, immorality among the brethren, lawsuits among believers, sexual immorality, inappropriate understandings of marriage, food being sacrificed to idols, propriety in worship and the Lord's Supper, and exercising of spiritual gifts. He brings all of it out into the open, inviting the church in Corinth to embrace its brokenness and lean fully into restoration, redemption and renewal. Only then will they become healthy and whole.

The apex of Paul's first letter to the Corinthian church leaders is chapter 13. It is most often read at marriage ceremonies—and appropriately so, since the "love chapter" is chock full of words and phrases to be displayed in our marriages and homes—but Paul's original intention was to invite the leaders and the entire community of faith in Corinth to live as one in Christ in this "most excellent way." Instead of competitively hyping or disregarding one another's particular gifts to the fellowship and continuously living in a state of disunity, Paul urges them to move beyond their differences into a harmony defined by love.

> And now I will show you the most excellent way. . . . Love is patient, love is kind. It does not envy, it does not boast, it is not proud. It is not rude, it is not self-seeking, it is not easily angered, it keeps no record of wrongs. Love does not delight in evil but rejoices with the truth. It always protects, always trusts, always hopes, always perseveres. Love never fails. . . . And now these three remain: faith, hope and love. But the greatest of these is love. (1 Corinthians 13:1, 4-8, 13)

We will explore together the sixteen words or phrases Paul uses to describe the most excellent way of love (from 1 Corinthians 13), and we will look at the dark undersides of each phrase to identify our propensity toward brokenness and weakness as distortions of God's love. When we discover that God is truly and forever love, then our restoration and transformation process belongs solely to him. When we learn to surrender to God as love and begin to live into his redemptive love, we embrace both our strengths and our brokenness and lead others in a radically different way.

At the end of each chapter you will be encouraged to confess your own brokenness and engage in a soul audit that invites your truthful response. Here you will discover the value of time spent in self-reflection, considering how best to "be still, and know that I am God" (Psalm 46:10). And in this spacious place of stillness you will know how, as Richard Meux Benson, founder of the Society of Saint John the Evangelist, once said, "the Spirit accommodates Himself to our littleness that we may expand to

His greatness." In that process you will begin to know yourself and those you serve with a greater depth of insight and wisdom. In addition, you will be encouraged to prayerfully consider how God is inviting you to assess your current ways of living in order to embrace a new way of following Jesus and leading others in his name.

Along the way I urge you to be gentle with your honesty, faithful in your authenticity and hopeful in your redemption. The confessions ahead of us will be good for our souls. Let's leave behind our hiding and hopelessness and enter the pathway to the abundant life of Christian leadership and followership with prayerful anticipation and joyful expectation.

- one -

Impatience Isn't a Virtue

Love is patient and kind

IT TAKES A LOT TO BREAK DOWN and ultimately dismantle my patience. I tend to be easygoing, and I consider patience a trait every leader should aspire to reflect. At rare times, however, I'm surprised how short-fused I can become; I experience firsthand how impatience can show my profound lack of virtue as a man after God's heart.

I can often be more patient with my colleagues than I am with my family. Those dearest to me tend to get the brunt of my impatience, mostly because they happen to be with me more frequently during the worst times of my day, when I'm more tired and cranky, or because familiarity actually can at times breed disdain and result in unkindness. However, it wasn't very long ago when I nearly lost my patience with a team I was leading. I had been betrayed by one of the members, and I was attempting to resolve the issue as swiftly as possible—but to no avail.

The betrayal came in the form of a misrepresentation of a conflicting philosophy between another ministry leader and me. I was being accused of not being open-minded about alternative personnel strategy and growth models. Even after meeting with those involved, I was alone in my conviction about what was most appropriate.

After seeking resolution on the matter several times, even meeting one on one with my primary adversary, I sought the counsel of others on the team. There was hesitancy in stepping into the issue with me, even if they were in agreement with me. It was complicated by the fact that my primary antagonist was involved in many other ministry settings and, further, that my challenger was a ministry leader with a vested interest in a much larger, more prestigious organization.

The particular team member who betrayed me had been a long-standing advocate of my leadership. He had voiced words of encouragement on several occasions. In our shared leadership experiences that spanned a decade of effectiveness, there were countless times where he publically affirmed my leadership. But this time he believed I had crossed the line. This time I disagreed with the wrong person: one of his closest friends. And I was confronted bitterly, rebuked harshly.

And I lost my patience.

Without much room to vent my frustration and inner anguish, I kept reaching out to others for strength and support. My heart was aching, my mind was confused, my work was affected and my relationships began to suffer. The very team I had spent oodles of time building was now beginning to splinter and unravel around the edges.

As a leader, I know this is serious stuff not to be avoided or brushed aside for any reason. But this time, it seemed much more complicated, and it became one of the most difficult leadership challenges I had faced up to that time in my leadership career. As my patience was tested and worn thin in this crucible of community, I realized I was beginning to show signs of exhaustion and frustration in my interactions with others. Questions from others that previously were rather innocent now became laced with (unnecessarily and unintended) suspicious and darker meaning. I became anxious and frustrated in a setting where I had previously been very much at home. In meetings and conversations I would allow myself to entertain unnecessary paranoia: *What was she really getting at by that comment or question?* It wasn't pretty.

I sought the advice of a trained counselor. His concluding comment at the end of our first meeting together floored me: "The goal of our sessions will be for you to see this painful relational experience as a gift from God." I immediately thought *he* was the irrational one! Little did I realize at that moment, his was the comforting voice of the redeeming Lord Jesus Christ who would see to it that my impatience would be redeemed for God's glory. His words would eventually come true. To this day I'm grateful for this incident. It forced me to come to grips with my immature impatience and to see it as a weakness that could only be turned to strength by the grace and goodness of God.

Within months of that patience-trying season, I was thanking God for the pain and suffering associated with what had been an incredible disappointment and betrayal. As the love of God began to flood my soul, I began to heal from the inside out. The incident came to an abrupt end, thanks be to God. The lessons to be learned had begun to dig deeply into my consciousness. Much of the perceived betrayal and critique of me that ensued had kernels of truth for me to prayerfully consider. The relationships were eventually healed and restored, although not to their pre-conflict state. Ultimately the experience made me a much stronger leader.

My impatience had been curbed by the grace, love and mercy of God. Patience had been restored from the depth of my soul's well. I came to know experientially what "Love is patient" truly means, but only by discovering that God himself is patient, and God gently encourages me toward patience too. His patience toward me generated patience toward those who disappointed or disagreed with me. At the same time I discovered afresh that "Love is kind," and through God's kindness I too can be both a recipient and dispenser of the kindness of God with those I am called to serve and lead. The long-suffering love of God is what enables me to be patient and kind as a leader.

LOVE IS PATIENT AND KIND

Patience and kindness go hand in glove. When the apostle Paul was writing to the church in Corinth about the most excellent way of love, he begins, appropriately, with patience: love is patient. He similarly describes the evidence of the Spirit in the heart of a believer as "patience" (Galatians 5:22) and encourages their patience amidst particular leadership challenges (Romans 5:3; 15:5; Ephesians 4:1-2; 1 Thessalonians 5:14). Love is also kind. To be kind is to exhibit a grace toward another, and even to oneself, that exudes both warmth and protection. To do so is to offer an embrace of loving-kindness and fortification against any attack that would seek to destroy love among others. Kindness is soft and bold, merciful and strong, compassionate and courageous.

In the church in Corinth many issues were not appropriately addressed due to a lack of kindness. These issues included schisms in the church, false understandings of what ministry looks like, intellectual pride, social issues, internal strife, sexual immorality, marital troubles, lawsuits and idolatry, just to name a few. Paul faced being discredited and dishonored himself by those who were leaders in the church, so he opens his heart and discloses his true motivations, spiritual passion and tender love for them. He does this with patience and kindness.

There was no backing down for Paul; he fulfilled his role among them with courageous determination, knowing the great need to preserve the church at all costs. The changes that needed to be made would be a radical departure from the way they had been addressing the issues.

Paul's example of godly leadership in the midst of relational strife and worldliness is one we must pay attention to today in our respective lives, relationships and ministries. Like so many others since biblical times, Paul was bold and dauntless in speaking directly into the impatient mean-spiritedness of the Corinthians. He defended his role as an apostle among them, spoke truthfully and lovingly into each and every issue they were facing, and invited them continuously and directly into a more excellent way—loving patience and kindness.

In 1 Corinthians 12, Paul encourages the Corinthian believers to be united as a body and not only to appreciate each other's spiritual gifts but also affirm the need for and importance of each gift. Celebrating one another can require a lot of patience. Since he knew of their propensity toward annoyance with one another and impatient irritation, he stresses the importance of endurance and respect. He highlights the weaker members of the body and deems the lesser ones of greater importance than the body parts that are most visible. In essence, he turns their previous way of being present in disunity upside down. He encourages them instead to embrace a new way of serving one another and the immoral people of Corinth as the life-giving body of Christ, in the most excellent way of love.

This way of encouraging them to be united as a body was a bold invitation. Paul knew that the only way the gospel would be advanced was through a united body. To try and accomplish all that was before them in such a pagan ministry setting in any other way would not have worked. He knew that as Jesus prayed for unity among his followers in John 17, so too would the church in Corinth be healthy and vibrant only if they were one in Christ. He appeals to them for such unity and calls them to reignite their passion for the gospel message as appropriately manifest in their life together: in marriages, worship, leadership and through their generosity. His call was for an openhanded way of living and being the people of God.

A patient exhibition of kindness is the call of God on all who claim his name and embrace his mission. But when push comes to shove (figuratively and even literally at times), since we are sinful, mortal humans, we don't always lean in that direction. Instead, we more naturally default to the spirit of impatient meanness. Are you willing to own your occasional propensity toward such meanness, whether mild or harsh, voiced or merely thought? What about when a frustration, anxiety or fear emerges from within and is acted out toward others in unusually irrational ways?

Patient love comes only from God. We cannot muster up or will ourselves to patience. God has expressed patience to us over and over and over again. So who else to turn to when we're in need of patience but God?

If I had trusted in God's patience in the leadership scenario above, I would have saved myself and others so much unnecessary pain. My impatience trumped God's patience. I was more determined to be right than to be patiently molded more into God's righteousness. Had I invited God's patient love to flow in and through me, the circumstances would have been dramatically different. Instead, I focused on my indignant need to be right, and it took months (instead of moments) for that to be corrected. Kindness would have gone a long way toward mitigating my impatience, and a lot of unnecessary relational damage could have been avoided.

INVITATION TO PATIENCE AND KINDNESS

There are endless options for how leaders are tested in their patience. Consider how your relationships, responsibilities, temperament and circumstances within or outside of your control affect your personal patience quotient. What category taps into your own impatient leanings?

Some leaders find that *family relationships* are the most challenging. Impatience can emerge among spouses, with parents, between siblings, toward children and in what can appear to be endless numbers of potential extended family squabbles. Talk to any leader today and you'll soon discover brokenness and at least one deeply painful family relationship, the ripple effects of which can sour their service to others.

Your *team* is another environment for potential conflict and resulting impatience. Teams are the place where leaders interact most intimately within their particular context of service and relational connection. Teams can either be united or divided, life-giving or life-draining, effective or stalled. Learning how best to lead a healthy team with patience and kindness is the finest antidote to a challenging team experience. As the leader goes, so goes the team.

Some leaders find that *individuals the team is serving* can also produce a spirit of impatience. A leader doesn't generally have a say over who will receive the services provided by one's team. Therefore, challenging personalities will ultimately come the way of a leader and can cause her to respond in ways that aren't always appropriate. Impatience can emerge rather quickly for a leader when faced with such people. We all have difficult personalities in our orbit; how do you deal with them and the accompanying brokenness they carry?

Leaders who have *responsibilities* that don't always match their gifts or passion can become impatient with the work before them. Examples of this include writing reports when one feels inadequate to do so or dealing with a conflict one isn't equipped to handle or drawing up a budget when one is not good with numbers. In these situations leaders can easily exhibit impatience with themselves. What are the tasks within your job description that elicit impatience from or toward yourself?

Leaders' *temperament* and the temperament of those with whom they serve can elicit impatience, for reasons often unknown to those involved. It's helpful when leaders have a good handle on their own personality strengths and temperament and knows these aspects of the people on their team as well. However, there are many times when even a baseline knowledge of temperament doesn't hinder an impatient response.

Adding complexity to our relationships, responsibilities and temperament are the *circumstances* within or beyond a leader's control. When, for example, there are mechanical difficulties with microphones, lights, audio-visual equipment or technology during a meeting or presentation, impatience can quickly emerge. Or when there is a crisis in one's larger community context that hinders one's work (such as extreme inclement weather conditions or an economic downturn across the nation), choosing a patient response can be difficult for many leaders.

Along with the broader circumstances that surround leaders are the personal *life situations* they have experienced. We are such complex individuals, with a mixture of broken experiences that have formed and shaped our current internal condition. Our hearts and souls are affected by the heartaches and painful experiences of life. We're also shaped by the happier highlights of our lives that feed our gratitude quotient for the many blessings God has so generously bestowed upon us. Both the personal circumstances and those that are beyond our control can and do hinder our ability to lead. Having a healthy awareness of our authentic reality—the good, the bad and the ugly—remains the best starting point for the way forward.

What would it look like for patience and kindness to reside in your heart and be restored in your life today?

First, consider what arouses a mean-spirited response from within. Most likely the reason for such a reply is far deeper than the immediate situation and potentially something that's been ignored for a very long time. When I sense such a comeback emerging in me, it is tied to an attitude or action that has long been troublesome to my heart and soul. Usually it stems from a feeling of being slighted or taken for granted or, worse yet, being disregarded, dismissed or ignored. An unkind response can come from all sorts of places in our hearts and is often connected to a wound that's yet to be healed.

Ironically, it's often the "disease of niceness" that allows for such meanness to occur in the first place. When ungodly behaviors and activities are initially encountered, where is the discipline to put a stop to them immediately? More times than we care to admit, a fear of hurting someone's feelings keeps us from truth telling and trust building in many leadership and relational contexts. We have come to believe, for whatever reason, that "it's not nice" to confront or discipline another. But when meanness is allowed to continue behind the scenes and even out in the open, others allow their own humanity to emerge, contributing to relational destruction as well. Instead of defaulting to grace and kindness, which includes a little strictness in order to safeguard love in the community of faith, they default to a more sinful posture of self-centered mean-spiritedness. And that produces a downward spiral and a complex mess that far too often is simply swept under the rug—the cause of ongoing conflict, which occurs in far too many settings.

Certain tones of voice can evoke an unpleasant response. Tones of anger or frustration, indignation or anxiety, even uncertainty and doubt can cause us to be tripped up. Pettiness, vulgarity and small mindedness convey meanness that to many is untenable. Listening to gossip and envy, displayed in petty conversation, tends to hurt all who participate. Vulgarity is simply embarrassing and disgusting, but amazingly can reproduce itself quite quickly if left unchecked by those in earshot of such words. Small mindedness comes out in judgmental attitudes from those who are usually the most grossly uninformed. The power of words and phrases used inappropriately can bring out a mean streak that's not only visible but audible and, as a result, can cause damaging relational collateral.

Being ostracized, bullied or mistreated by others are yet more forms of meanness among people. Unfortunately, the Christian community is not exempt. Social media and new social mores can provoke such bullying, which can lead to feelings of insecurity. Who is guarding the hearts of adults who are experiencing this kind of ostracism and exclusion? Such mistreatment seems like it's become epidemic today, and Christian families, churches and ministry teams often find themselves in these traumatizing situations.

Injustice toward a weaker member of society is another form of mean-spiritedness. It's amazing to observe how often responses to injustice mirror the mean-spiritedness of the perpetrator. We must be careful to respond with loving-kindness and avoid escalating the injustice we are seeking to resolve.

Unwillingness to come to the table and reconcile and forgive is another form of mean-spiritedness. When a person is invited to participate in restoring brokenness and refuses to do so, that can be interpreted as a form of relational injustice. The work of reconciliation is hard enough, but to have someone unwilling to engage in that effort breeds a spirit of unkindness that is cancerous. Too many marriages, families, churches, workplaces and ministries are strapped with this unfortunate reality. Leaders need to do everything possible to be reconcilers and restorers of justice, beginning with their own roles and responsibilities.

Outright meanness and malevolence can bring forth unkindness in return. Avoiding such a retort requires discipline from within; it can't always be controlled by legislating change or demanding a different way of being present with one another. Frankly, the only way kindness can be restored is through the love of God, specifically the *kind* love of God.

Within the body of Christ, kindness is best exhibited in healthy relationships. Therefore, the gifts that accompany *hospitality* go a long way toward the cultivation of hearts and lives that offer and receive a genuine and welcoming spirit of inclusion. When we create such an atmosphere, we discover the joy of *spiritual friendship* that provokes kindness and goodness within us and in our relationships. In the context of *community* we are given multiple opportunities to lead others into relational and emotional vitality; this includes both the ways we build relationships and the ways we maintain relationships, even when sternness is needed to resolve conflict.

So, regardless of the list of items that can induce an impatient response, what is God's invitation for his leaders today? As noted by the apostle Paul, it's best to befriend our impatience and look at it prayerfully, seeking to understand why impatience and meanspiritedness were the response. Selecting a more patient and gracious reply will bring our leadership back to the center and restore a harmonious climate. Trusting the God of patient love to equip us with patient love is the best way forward—and the most reliable. Patient love matched with kindness resembles God much more than the alternatives we inadvertently select on our own.

Spiritual Leadership Audit

Restoring Patience and Kindness

Creating sacred space to reflect on the concepts developed in this chapter will aid your ability to own your brokenness and recall the times when impatience or unkindness emerged in your heart and was expressed with your attitudes, words or actions. Take some time in prayer to reflect on the chapter you've just read. When the apostle Paul reminds his readers that "love is patient" and "love is kind," we need to pay attention to our immediate or internal response. What is your heart inclined toward when impatient mean-spiritedness is demonstrated by others or emerges from within you? Don't glide over these questions too quickly; invest in a few moments of quiet reflection using the questions and texts below to guide you into patience and kindness by the God of patient loving-kindness.

Confess your brokenness: Naming your brokenness and owning it as a present reality.

- In what way(s) have you found yourself impatient or mean-spirited, or experienced impatience or mean-spiritedness from another, most recently?

- Consider prayerfully the details of this experience and recount them here.

Rest and trust in God's abiding presence and peace: Asking for God's patience and kindness to be revealed and released from within your soul.

- *Hopeful in Scripture:* Consider prayerfully James 5:7-11, and invite God to reveal his patient intention for you. Then read Ephesians 4:29-32 to reveal his intention for you to be kind to others.

- *Faithful in prayer:* Inquire of the Lord in regard to a specific person, responsibility, temperament or circumstance that evokes your impatience or mean-spiritedness, and seek his wisdom for offering a more patient and kind response. Is there reconciliation needed?

- *Thankful in reflection:* Identify with more detail and in prayerful contemplation how you plan to develop a more patient and kind disposition under the loving hand and fresh empowerment of God's Spirit.

Invite God to redeem your brokenness: Restoring God's loving patience and kindness in you. Attending to our impatience and mean-spiritedness and intending instead to embody God's patience and loving-kindness:

- Identify ways you have reverted to impatience (or mean-spiritedness) as a reaction to the person, responsibility or circumstance that most often provokes you. What do you notice? To whom and for what must you apologize today?

- Consider afresh the importance of Sabbath rest and the implications for rest as it relates to your impatience. When has God ever been in a rush to create or re-create something or someone of beauty? As you *cease* your normal workweek activities, *rest* in a quiet and reflective way, *celebrate* your life in God and community, and *embrace* your identity in Christ, how will this soften your heart and allow patience to emerge? Adrenaline-free rest may be the best choice for an impatient soul.

- Reflect on the significance of spiritual friendship and the implications for developing godly community as it relates to your need for the kindness of God. How is his loving-kindness residing deep within your heart and soul even today? How could you receive and/or express loving-kindness proactively to one of your spiritual friends today? How can you exhibit God's loving-kindness toward all who cross your path today?

- two -

When Envy and Jealousy Ransack the Mind

Love does not envy

FOR LENT ONE YEAR I GAVE UP all forms of social media. It simply had become too toxic for me. For the first few months of the year I found myself spending far too much time reading Facebook posts, searching for additional material about other organizations like ours and fixating on the accomplishments of others. What transpired within me was a growing envy and jealousy that was eating away at the fabric of my soul.

Constantly monitoring social media caused a subtle corrosion of a deeply spiritual self-awareness and replaced it with a growing fear of not measuring up. But what was the measuring stick, and who was I envying? Where had this fear come from, and why was I allowing it to take root in my heart and soul? The wake-up call was slow in coming; for several weeks I remained unaware of the negative effects of listening to all the wrong voices in my head convincing me our ministry wasn't excelling rapidly enough.

Over a decade ago, God led my wife and me out of a very healthy, stable ministry environment to start a brand new organization: Leadership Transformations. Taking the plunge into the world of ministry entrepreneurship was something we were not accustomed to doing. In fact, looking back, this decision was the largest risk of our lives—and one of the best decisions we've ever made as a family.

God was behind and ahead of this from the start. He was the one who gave me the dream and woke me up very early one August morning in 2002 with an obvious and unique call on my life. He was the one who companioned us through a prayerful discernment process that resulted in the decision to launch Leadership Transformations (LTI). He was the one who led others to come alongside us to weigh all the options with us and take this giant leap of faith. Yes, God was the one who invited us into his will, and he was the one who would keep opening doors every step of the way. LTI is God's ministry, blessed and multiplied by his gracious and generous hand, and the ministry has been utilized for his glory over and over again.

So why was I in such a vulnerable state in the winter of our eleventh year of service, on the heels of another successful and upwardly effective year of ministry, which included a huge ten-year anniversary celebration? The only way I can account for the state of my soul at that time is exhaustion. To look beyond my physical and emotional exhaustion at that time would have been to introduce the work of the enemy of my soul. If I began to question God's call or allow myself to believe false voices of self-condemnation and shame or see all of our previous work as a failure, I would have traveled down a dark road leading to despair. And if I willingly considered the voice of ridicule and diminution of the obvious-to-everyone-else (and, on my good days, obvious to me too) blessings from God, the enemy would have held a tight grip on my heart and mind. Exhaustion and enemy attack make for a vulnerable and unhealthy soul.

Envy rears its ugly head when we're not in a good place internally. We become envious toward another when we aren't feeling very good about ourselves. We look over our shoulders and into the lives of others when we aren't at a place of inner contentment and joy. Envy is accompanied by her friend jealousy, and when combined, they make for ugly companionship in the soul. It's not a fun state, and we often hide it from those who could in fact love us out of that horrible emotional place. So we plod along in our misery instead, with envy eating away at the root of our heart and soul.

As I was perusing social media and seeing numbers of likes, lists of accomplishments, new activities, beautiful photos and self-aggrandized accolades, I simply could not find room in my heart to rejoice over any of it. Instead, I began to despise what I was seeing in others' lives, so dramatically portrayed for all to see. The more time I spent online, the more I began to realize how much ill will this was causing in my soul. I was weeping as others were rejoicing, rather than rejoicing with them. I wanted out, and the only way to distance myself from my envy was to cease all forms of such activity and find respite for my weary soul.

Stopping all forms of social media connection, especially Facebook, was the best decision for me. It allowed me to flush out of my heart and mind all forms of waste that had accumulated as a blockade to my spiritual health and well-being. This purging brought about a much-needed perspective-building season of examination, confession and cleansing for my soul. Ceasing the activities that foster an envying heart and mind is a necessary prerequisite to recalibration of the soul. The result was a renewed intimacy with Christ and the ability to receive the loving affirmation from him that my heart was longing for.

God's desire for the body of Christ today, as for the early church and specifically the church in Corinth, is for envy to be dissipated by love. That was God's desire for Cain and Abel, Joseph and his brothers, Jacob and Esau, Rachel and Leah, and Saul and David, just to name a few biblical characters who give us insight into this common problem for God's people. When we see this issue in a larger perspective we realize we're in good company. Envy isn't something new; no, it's been the experience for many—if not most—of God's children since the dawn of time.

LOVE DOES NOT ENVY

When Paul writes to the Corinthian church leaders about love as the highest and most excellent way of leading others, he states clearly that love isn't envious. From the opening verses of 1 Corinthians, Paul is clearly stating that he's writing to the single, united church in Corinth, those sanctified in Christ Jesus and called to be holy, together with those everywhere who call on the name of the Lord Jesus Christ (1 Corinthians 1:2). In Paul's mind, there was to be no separation among them. Twice (1 Corinthians 1:12; 3:1-9) he notes how he's heard of their division, which springs from those who follow Paul or Apollos or Cephas, when in fact they are all to follow Christ. These factions create envy, strife and discord. Instead, Paul reminds them that whoever plants or waters the seed needs God, who makes things grow. Therefore, he urges them to rid themselves of any such envy and division and instead remain fertile for God to accomplish all of his purposes in their midst. This is Paul's first example of how envy spoils the love of God and separates the people of God.

Envy eats away at the core of love and is not an acceptable way to relate to one another. Envy, and the accompanying covetousness and jealousy, is in opposition to love in many disparaging ways. The bottom line: envy destroys at all times. "A heart at peace gives life to the body, but envy rots the bones" (Proverbs 14:30).

Although often lumped together, envy, covetousness and jealousy are quite distinct from one another. *Envy* is a longing for something that currently isn't yours and the begrudging feeling of discontent, dislike or ill will toward the person who possesses that which you desire. *Covetousness* stretches out the envy toward that which is not yours and is completely outside your ability to attain it. *Jealousy* is the fear of losing something or someone that you feel currently belongs to you; it's very careful to guard that belonging and can become resentful or zealously envious if the belonging is ever threatened or lost.

The biblical sin of envy is most closely associated with covetousness. For example, we are commanded not to covet our neighbor's wife. When we covet, we are resentful that our neighbor has her and we don't, whereas, if she was ours first, then we become jealous that she's now in someone else's embrace. Envy comes from the Latin word *invidere*, which means "to look askance upon" or, in a more common vernacular, to give the other the "evil eye" of malice or spite. Although considered "nicer" than jealousy, in fact envy isn't as benign as some might suspect. It's a horrible heart disease no matter how we slice it or define it.

Envy simply doesn't belong in the heart of a leader, or any person who believes in Christ and seeks to honor him in their life and service to others. We are commanded not to covet or envy anything that isn't ours. "You shall not covet your neighbor's house. You shall not covet your neighbor's wife, or his manservant or maidservant, his ox or donkey, or anything that belongs to your neighbor" (Exodus 20:17). Envy and coveting enfold us when we spend our time looking over our shoulders at

another's relationships, experiences or possessions. When our
eyes are looking at someone else's life, they are certainly not
looking in the right direction—whether upward to God, inward
toward self-knowledge or outward toward service of others.

From my experience in leadership within several ministry
contexts serving in staff, board and volunteer roles, I have
noticed that envy has various sources within the heart and mind
of the believer. Each of these sources creates a feeling about oneself that opens the door for envy to take root and bear fruit
in the lives and relationships of Christian leaders. As you consider the following you might want to jot notes in the margin
about the ways these have crept into your journey as well.

One such source of envy is *insecurity*, which is based in fear.
An insecure leader is fearful of not measuring up to what's
expected or implied by others, or fed and grown from within.
Out of such insecurity comes a propensity to envy those who
seem like they are much better off, in stature as a leader, in status among your peers, or in situations where numbers, programs
and success seem to be the fruitful result of effectiveness. The
insecure person often does not feel very good about what's hap-
pening in or around them, whether the assessment of reality is
true or false. Insecurity can on the one hand suspend a leader
from forward movement or, on the other end of the spectrum,
cripple a leader from any movement whatsoever. All of this is
based in unmerited fear, which can only be healed by love.

Another source of envy is *inaccuracy*, which is rooted in
assumption. When we lead others, beginning with ourselves, and
we do so with inaccurate information as our baseline, we end up
in the geography of misperception. In this place we tend to look
at all aspects of ministry from a skewed perspective. We make
inaccurate assumptions, which leads to disappointment, and
when we're in that place emotionally we are more inclined to look

at others with envy. It takes work to listen attentively and respond accordingly. But one way out of the sin of envy is accurate assessment, which, more times than not, can result in loving appreciation for what *is* rather than wishing for something else.

An additional source of envy is *instability*, which is often based in a bias or prejudice. When leaders are in a place of relative instability—either not feeling good about their role or in a hot seat of criticism—the uncertainty can evoke envy and covetousness. Our biases or prejudices emerge out of a conviction that one person is right and the other is wrong, and they can often curb our ability to look at things from a solidly balanced perspective. The longer the instability lasts, the more deeply entrenched the prejudices can become. Such views of self, others or the situations we find ourselves in can certainly hinder the leader's effectiveness. Only love reveals and releases our propensity toward a specific bias.

INVITATION TO RELEASE ENVY

Envy and her close relatives covetousness and jealousy can wreak havoc on the soul of a God-honoring life. When we are so concerned about our right to be in the center of activities and on the heart and mind of others, we are striving to be recognized for the value we bring to relationships and situations. When we don't get the recognition we desire, we look longingly and enviably to those who are receiving the applause we feel we most deserve. Or, when we desire more than anything to gain in reputation or accumulation of assets or accolades, we begin to manipulate our way toward the achievement of our personal agenda. Then we look critically at other people's success with a heart of envy and strife. The energy we exert toward self-protection and self-aggrandizement is exhausting, yet we

continue to pursue center stage and push others out of the lime-
light in order to be recognized at all cost.

This yearning for status, recognition, accomplishment and
acquisition ends up driving us into a state of instability. As a
result, we cannot serve with open and outstretched hands of love
toward others. Instead we simply seek to receive, and find it quite
challenging, if not impossible, to share much of anything with
others. Once envy has a grip on our soul, we flail around purpose-
lessly and inadvertently hurt others in the process. When we
struggle with envy we can be so enveloped by self that to consider
the needs of others more important than our own is nigh to
impossible. We are trapped in envy and become unteachable or,
worse yet, we risk imploding and possibly losing that which we
treasure most.

Isn't it time to embrace your occasional propensity toward
envy, confess your need for God's grace and lean more fully into
the antidotes of what can be debilitating covetousness? If you
find yourself always wanting to look good, or you seem to continuously examine others with a critical eye, then considering a
new way of leading may be for you. If you think you're not being
treated fairly or suffer from a sense of inferiority, then it's time
to replace feelings of inadequacy with godly self-awareness and
a new way of leading and loving without envy.

The place to begin is *clarity* about your current reality. Placing
a mirror out in front to observe yourself with God-honoring
eyes allows you to see yourself as you really are. When you view
yourself from God's lens of love and affection, then you can
receive yourself as a dearly loved child of the heavenly Father. If
you need help from another observer, then ask a spiritual friend,
guide or director to offer you a godly vantage point. Seeing,
accepting and embracing our reality helps us to let go of the
need to envy the status or situation of another. Defining one's

reality is always the leader's first stop on the train to healthy effectiveness. Making sure you listen to the right voice(s) is the place to begin achieving godly clarity.

Growing out of that keen awareness is an inner sense of *contentment* and peace, knowing that no matter what may come our way, choosing serenity in God will lead us back home to joy. Like the apostle Paul in his prison cell, we too can cry out with delight, "I have learned to be content whatever the circumstances. I know what it is to be in need, and I know what it is to have plenty. I have learned the secret of being content in any and every situation, whether well fed or hungry, whether living in plenty or in want. I can do everything through him who gives me strength" (Philippians 4:11-13). Learning the secret of contentment will lead you off the pathway of envy and back onto the road to love, peace and joy.

Companionship is the third resource for warding off envy. We need one another as believers and peers to speak truth into our souls about the true nature of God and the true nature of ourselves in God. Our spiritual friends are the extension of God's loving arms and his tender voice of companionship offered to us through the ministry of the Holy Spirit. We are not designed to live in isolation from the body of Christ. Instead, as members of God's household we are called on to breathe life, hope and vitality into one another's hearts. Spiritual friends are those who affirm and celebrate the unique person you are and seek to generate ways for you to flourish. Who among us doesn't need the companionship of the Holy Spirit expressed through his chosen vessels of love and grace?

Additionally, a fourth resource to lean on is *compassion*, first toward ourselves and then emanating outward into every other relationship. Having patience and compassion in our process of maturation will pour life, health and strength into our heart and soul. Developing a compassionate heart leads us away from envy and into the embrace of love. When we offer a compassionate heart toward those in our relationship circles, we are in essence serving others in Jesus' name.

Spiritual Leadership Audit

Restoring Your Contentment

Has this chapter evoked any internal response, which, if skipped over, would mean missing something crucial for yourself or those you love and serve? The opposite of contentment is envy, so to identify when and with whom we find ourselves envious is critical to our ongoing pursuit of spiritual health and vitality. It's not the prettiest of places to go in one's heart and soul for sure, since envy is one of our more ugly responses. But we all struggle with this to one extent or another. So press the pause button for a few moments and sit with the following questions and activities and see what emerges as a result. Let God jealously receive your full self so that his envy-free love can rise up from within your soul and spill out onto yourself and others you are called to love and serve in Jesus' name.

Confess your brokenness: Naming your brokenness and owning it as a present reality.

- In what way(s) have you found yourself envious, or experienced envy from another, most recently?

- Consider prayerfully the details of this experience and recount them here.

Rest and trust in God's abiding presence and peace: Seeking God's contentment to be revealed and released from within your soul.

- *Hopeful in Scripture:* Spend some time reflecting on Paul's imprisonment and his secret of contentment as noted in Philippians 4:10-13.

- *Faithful in prayer:* Invite the Spirit of God to enlighten your awareness of how you long to be healed of your envy by the compassionate love of the Father toward you, his beloved child.

- *Thankful in reflection:* Consider when you most recently struggled with envy toward another. How would you envision being freed from this disordered attachment? What steps would you need to take?

   Invite God to redeem your brokenness: Restoring God's loving contentment in you. Attending to our envy as a leader and intending instead to embody God's enviable love in our leadership:

- Contentment is the key to breaking the power of envy. Take a block of time to journal or draw out the many ways God has blessed your life and has shown himself to be faithful to you. As you see the myriad gifts he has offered to you, give voice to your gratitude and ask God to help you discover the secret of contentment once more.

- Envy will cripple you emotionally if you let it maintain a grip on your heart. Having a growing awareness of your vulnerable spots for envy and covetousness will aid you in your spiritual growth. How will you contemplatively practice the discipline of noticing God at work within you while you attend to your propensity to envy? Feed and foster the discipline of noticing God in this and all other areas of your with-God life.

- three -

Is It Ever Acceptable to Have
a Competitive Spirit?

Love does not boast

THE WORD *COMPETITION* DOESN'T APPEAR in the English
Bible. Further, there isn't a Hebrew or Greek term that the
Scriptures reference to build on its importance, with the exception of terms like *rivalry, vanity, boasting* and *conceit*. But, competition certainly exists in the body of Christ, whether we
choose to recognize it or not. And it resides in your heart and
mine, if we're honest enough to admit it.

Competition's net effect is always negative and, at worst,
destructive to all who are entangled by its lure. And yet competition is such a prevalent aspect of many churches and ministries today, mostly because it exists in us—the very persons who
make up our organizations.

A few years ago a Christian online marketing group set up a
contest among ministries with a grand prize of $50,000. The
contest was set up with the hope of finding the *best* ministry
making the *most* life change somewhere in the world. The campaign organizers got ministries to submit an application and

then encouraged them to solicit their respective ministry members and friends to go online and vote for them. The one with the most votes won the big bucks, with second- and third-place winners receiving lesser but still very significant amounts.

This unique approach to distribution of funds to ministries troubled my soul from the day I first heard about it. Our ministry was asked to be in the beta test group. We denied the request. I sent in my comments, even voiced my concerns to one of the organizers on the phone. But to no avail. The contest was launched and several organizations entered. A few ministry announcements about the contest entered my inbox and I was one of those invited via email to quickly go and vote for one ministry vying for the big prize. Each time I heard about this contest, I had a check in my spirit and a lump in my throat.

There were a few rounds of these "competitions" for ministry dollars that followed the first one. Truth be told, we finally joined one of the later campaigns when the organizers softened the competitive language and flattened the size and number of gifts offered. Instead of promoting a competitive advantage between and against one another, the funding entity simply encouraged ministries like ours to consider using their online giving platform to increase awareness about our ministry. They matched the dollars we raised online in a given time frame and affirmed the importance of our ministry—and all the others— by dealing more fairly with every group who participated. Thankfully, what began as a boastful competition eventually settled into a mutually edifying encouragement to all, and I commend the organizers for making the switch.

Does any form of a boastful, competitive approach to serving others belong in the Christian community? For that matter, does competitive boasting of any stripe belong among Christians, churches or organizations? In the case of this one particularly blatant competition, it appeared to me that all should be winners since I didn't see anything that smacked of "loser" anywhere among their initial campaign applicants. Nor do I see *any* church or ministry as a loser. Period.

Whether we like it or not, a boastful and competitive spirit exists in the Christian church today. It's everywhere. Take, for example, the magazine that focuses annually on the "fastest growing and largest congregations in America"—how do you think that issue makes the pastor of a small, rural congregation feel about his tiny-sized flat-attendance mediocrity? Or the report that's generated about the growth of satellite churches among the largest congregations in America. Or the fundraising groups that advertise in Christian magazines about their largest capital campaigns. Or even the fact that book publishers, educational institutions, mission agencies and any number of other organizations that market themselves do so by referencing their competitive edge among their "peers" in their particular sector of the Christian marketplace? When have you ever seen an ad in a magazine that says, "After you've looked at others doing excellent work, and prayerfully considered God's distinct call, you may wish to come to our school/buy our resource/join our event"? Such marketing simply doesn't exist.

Never mind the fact that since the Reformation we've created over forty thousand denominations worldwide, all of which were formed out of "protest" (hence the term Protest-ant movement) in theology, personality or practice. Or the fact that there was a book published on the evangelical parachurch movement several years ago with a taxonomy in the back that went on for nearly two dozen pages listing all the different types of parachurch organizations in the world today. Why? Because we have an independent mindset that leads us to make choices that fit our best interests. Then we compete with one another to grab commitment and resources and involvement away from others. It's not always blatant and is certainly done with the best intentions, I might add. But it leads to negative and unintended consequences such as a competitive spirit of boasting and comparisons.

Our independent mindsets are what contribute most to the competition we see in the body of Christ today. We've been taught in our culture to take care of self, watch out for self, provide for self and even promote self. Our children today learn that there's no such thing as company loyalty in the business world. Instead, we urge them to be president and CEO of a company bearing their own name and make sure they aren't left "out there" to depend on anyone but themselves. Is it any wonder that self-protection and self-referencing are the modern-day version of boasting? It's hard to be in most conversations today without the occurrence of some form of self-referencing, that is, when my response to what I hear from another is more about my own perspective or vantage point than what the person has just verbalized.

Our independence and self-focus are destroying community and instead are building fences that keep us apart. In the body of Christ we've become competitors rather than cooperators. The biblical text offers zero evidence that competition should exist within the Christian community (with one exception: we all share one enemy, the devil, with whom we are in constant competition). In fact, quite the contrary.

The enemy of our souls—the *only* one we're to be in competition with—loves to stir up a competitive spirit among the body of Christ. And, unfortunately, competition exists everywhere you turn: among individual Christians, local churches, private schools, mission agencies and well-meaning organizations of varying shapes and sizes, all vying for what's perceived to be a scarcity of time, talent and treasure.

Most specifically, a spirit of competition resides within your heart and mine. If we're honest with one another, and ourselves, we struggle with a drive to be seen, heard and recognized more than others. Where are you most competitive today? Why? Confess that before the Lord, ask for his gracious forgiveness, and lean instead in the direction of openhanded generosity of heart, mind and will toward all who cross your path.

Instead of competition in the body of Christ I would suggest there is a higher calling. And it includes such virtues as gracious cooperation, patiently prayerful community, and an over-the-top generous commitment to one another no matter what. That's how and when the world will truly come to know Christ. This is the better—and most excellent—way.

Love Does Not Boast

Paul the apostle was very familiar with boasting. Before his dramatic conversion, he boasted arrogantly against all Christians. Now that he's writing to the church in Corinth, he's boldly expressing the fact that love must never include a boasting spirit. He continually warns against such conceited blustering. There is no room for competition in the body, especially in a place like Corinth, where the explicit ways people were living were more an expression of evil than good, sensuality rather than morality, godlessness instead of godliness. Paul continually urged the church in Corinth toward unity, grace, wisdom and propriety. His call was to invite the leaders of the church to join him in spreading everywhere the fragrance of the knowledge of God and the scent of life (2 Corinthians 2:14-17). All of this was to be done with an unwavering optimism and integrity, and without boasting about any success achieved.

Paul, knowing that ministry in Corinth was tough, reminds the leaders that "since through God's mercy we have this ministry, we do not lose heart. . . . We have renounced secret and shameful ways; we do not use deception, nor do we distort the word of God. . . . We have this treasure in jars of clay to show that this all-surpassing power is from God and not from us. . . . Therefore we do not lose heart" (2 Corinthians 4:1-2, 7, 16). Clay is easily breakable, so there is no room for boasting and swaggering, which destroy what God intends to complete. Only one boasting is acceptable: boasting in the Lord.

If we are to express love toward one another in the body of Christ, we must not boast. Such a relational tactic doesn't build community or trust. Boasting has always been frowned on, but many who boast don't even realize they are doing so. Even when boasting would be the last thing on our mind, we can end up speaking well of ourselves or our organizations and even our churches in a rather boastful way. We certainly don't mean to boast, but our enthusiasm takes over. Any time we're using superlatives (*highest, largest, longest, best, brightest, biggest*) to speak of ourselves or our organizations, we are boasting. There's a fine line between being boastful and self-centered versus grateful and verbally thankful for God's blessing. It's all about the posture and attitude of the heart.

When I'm with other ministry leaders, I need to watch how boisterous I am about how well things are going at LTI, especially when the person I'm with isn't in a healthy work environment. When my wife and I find a worshiping community that we enjoy, we spill over with delight in our honest reflections, but we need to be careful that we don't sound arrogant or boastful that "ours" is more holy, reverent and worshipful than "yours." When we talk to others about the amazing soul care group we're in and how much it's meant to us, we need to be cautious that it doesn't hurt another's feelings about their own small group experience. When we speak well of our children's latest accomplishments or our family's most recent vacation, we simply need to be sensitive to those hearing our glowing testimonies. We may be sharing with a couple that hasn't seen or experienced anything close to that in their own family system. Common sense and sensitive sharing are the foundation for meaningful and mutual relationships.

I'm convinced that much modern-day boasting among believers occurs more subtly as self-referencing than outright in-your-face self-glorification. It's in our natural, human propensity to consider our own experience(s) each time we're in conversation with others. But when we routinely respond by sharing from our experience, we simply draw attention back to ourselves.

The next time you're with your spouse, your child, your friend, your colleague, even a complete stranger, resist the urge to self-reference. Or, as the comedian Brian Regan puts it so humorously, "Beware the me monster," which is so readily inclined to out-boast all others within earshot. We're too sophisticated to be outright boastful about ourselves, so we've succumbed instead to the more moderate self-referencing. Yet it simply doesn't belong in the community of faith where others are to be consistently considered ahead of us. And, ironically, each time I raise this as an issue in the body of Christ it evokes responses like "No way! Not us!" or "It may not be okay in the church or ministry context, but it's 'necessary to have competition' in business, politics or sports." It's certainly a topic worthy of community exploration, prayerful consideration and ongoing self-evaluation.

Jesus spent a fair amount of time addressing the issue of boasting. He told a story about a Pharisee in which "the Pharisee stood up and prayed about himself: 'God, I thank you that I am not like all other men—robbers, evildoers, adulterers—or even like this tax collector. I fast twice a week and give a tenth of all I get'" (Luke 18:11-12). About the Scribes he says, "Beware of the teachers of the law. They like to walk around in flowing robes and love to be greeted in the marketplaces and have the most important seats in the synagogues and the places of honor at banquets. They devour widows' houses and for a show make lengthy prayers. Such men will be punished most severely" (Luke 20:46-47). Yet another time he addressed the manner in which people were giving: "As he looked up, Jesus saw the rich putting their gifts into the temple treasury. He also saw a poor widow put in two very small copper coins. 'I tell you the truth,' he said, 'this poor widow has put in more than all the others. All these people gave their gifts out of their wealth; but she out of her poverty put in all she had to live on'" (Luke 21:1-4).

Over and over again, Jesus confronts the religious leaders, the showboating disciples, the rich, the arrogant and the foolish, and he invites them to flee from their self-righteous ways and enter instead into a life of simple-hearted, behind-the-scenes, others'-centered righteousness that reflects the true heart of God. To live this way is to choose the blessed route of a merciful, peacemaking, and kingdom-building way of living—in other words, the opposite of self-conceited and arrogant boasting.

INVITATION TO JOY

When I entered the spiritual formation world, I truly thought I'd be leaving behind the wider and more competitive church and ministry world. Over time, I was shocked to discover that even in the realm of holiness and spiritual vitality there exists hard-driving, self-absorbed, competitively motivated leaders and teams. Including, at times, me.

Why I thought it would be any different in the sphere of spiritual formation is baffling. I was so naive and so fed up with the "old way" of church, ministry and parachurch competition that I truly had imagined a romanticized and idealistic world of others'-centered soul-based ministry life.

Imagine if instead of competitive boasting we chose cooperative community building. Imagine if instead of setting up top-down corporate climates within our organizations we chose to create loving community. Imagine if instead of viewing each other with a critical spirit we chose to affirm and celebrate one another. Imagine if instead of manipulating others toward our own agenda we chose to compliment one another. Imagine if instead of looking to our own interests in literally every arena of decision making we chose to consider others more important than ourselves. Imagine if instead of competing against each other we competed to be the first to out-love one another.

Imagine if pure, unhindered joy guided our life together. Imagine that for a moment. Joy. If joy were the guiding motivation of our lives, then instead of boasting and competing with one another, we would delight in, with and for others. We would rejoice with those who rejoice. We would weep with those who weep. Gone would be the weeping as others rejoice and the rejoicing when others weep. When joy is the light that illumines the heart and enlightens the path, then the journey ahead of us will be traveled with greater unity, healthier relationships and more purposeful commonality.

Choosing joy is an option for every believer, in spite of any and all of our life's genuinely realistic circumstances. As the prophet once pronounced, "Though the fig tree does not bud and there are no grapes on the vines, though the olive crop fails and the fields produce no food, though there are no sheep in the pen and no cattle in the stalls, yet I will rejoice in the LORD, I will be joyful in God my Savior. The Sovereign LORD is my strength; he makes my feet like the feet of a deer, he enables me to go on the heights" (Habakkuk 3:17-19).

Like the prophet Habakkuk, we too must learn how to rejoice in the Lord and find our joy in him alone, no matter the climate of our work or quality of our relationships. Making joy our preferred response to all that life brings our way will indeed enhance our attitude and deepen our peace—especially when competitive boasting comes our way or becomes the way of our own heart. Discovering and choosing joy is by far the best medicine for the soul.

What will it mean for joy to be restored within and around you as you live the abundant life and lead others accordingly? I'd like to suggest that our posture of boasting and competition be set free from the inside out so that we are detached from our self-referencing and instead are captivated by the joy of the Lord as our strength and song. To do so, we are much better served by making a conscious choice to consider others more important than ourselves. Choose joy by choosing freedom from the inside out:

- freedom from the need to be front and center

- freedom from the need to be head of the class and leader of the pack

- freedom from the need to be the smartest, most witty or articulate, and allow others the privilege of being heard first

- freedom from the need to be fastest and first, brightest and best

In essence, it's freedom to let go and let God, to release a competitive spirit and replace it with renewed joy in Jesus and with others in your community.

Spiritual Leadership Audit

Restoring Your Joy

A boastful, competitive attitude can be the death of a relationship and the demise of a heart. However, when the God of joyful love is filling up and overflowing a heart with his delight, then a cooperative and non-competitive spirit becomes evident. Isn't that your preference as a child of God and an emissary of his love, as a leader of others and a servant of Jesus? If so, then sit with these questions and reflection activities with an openness and receptivity to both confess your brokenness as a competitive person and embrace your calling as a person of joy. Living and leading from this posture will evoke fullness of life for you and for all who cross your path.

Confess your brokenness: Naming your brokenness and owning it as a present reality.

- In what way(s) have you found yourself boastful or competitive, or experienced boastfulness or competition from another, most recently?

- Consider prayerfully the details of this experience and recount them here.

Rest and trust in God's abiding presence and peace: Seeking God's joy to be revealed and released from within your soul.

- *Hopeful in Scripture:* Read through the book of Philippians and recall that this gospel of joy was written by Paul in a prison cell. Where do you find him espousing and/or most filled with joy? Note that there are nearly twenty references for joy included in the letter.

- *Faithful in prayer:* What is God's invitation for you during this season of life to disarm you from a boastful, competitive spirit and help you enter into a renewed time of joy?

- *Thankful in reflection:* Recall those times in your personal and professional life when you felt the most joy. What accompanied the joy in relationships, service or other life-giving experiences? Recount them with thanksgiving.

Invite God to redeem your brokenness: Restoring God's loving joy in you. Attending to our boastful/competitive spirit as a leader and intending instead to embody God's joy in my leadership:

- Take an "attachment inventory" of your personal and professional life. Ask yourself, *What attitude, personality trait, action, achievement or possession do I feel invited to release or hold more loosely?* Ask the Lord to replace that attachment with a reattached love and affection for Christ.

- Healthy detachment means having a "care less" attitude (still caring, but caring less in order to be involved at a healthier, more appropriately detached level) about that which has defined you as a person: your possessions, accomplishments, credentials, pedigree, even your personality, giftedness and acuity. What would life look like today if you simply held these more lightly and offered them more graciously, rather than holding fast to them and only releasing them when you felt it was time to manipulatively abandon their control?

- In what way(s) can you out-love another in Jesus' name today? In the week ahead? Are you willing to do so anonymously so that your love is unconditionally motivated and without any need for response?

- four -

The Tight Grip of Pride and Close-Fisted Greed

Love is not proud

I HONESTLY DON'T KNOW too many blatantly proud or overtly greedy leaders. Neither attribute is very amiable or endearing to convey to the public eye. To be so would undermine their role as a leader, particularly within the Christian ministry world. But when leaders are put under pressure or confronted by overwhelming odds, it's amazing how both pride *and* pride's tight-fisted cousin greed can rear their ugly heads.

I noticed this in myself at a recent professional conference I attended. We were there to discover insights from one another in a setting designed for a community of learners with shared leadership. All who were invited to attend had been recognized for their focus on the topic either as authors, speakers and/or practitioners. It was an honor and privilege to be invited, and with the invitation came complementary registration from the foundation supporting the event (can you already hear the pride bubbling up inside me?).

During one session I noticed that someone who had already spoken once had been invited to participate in a second panel designed for college and seminary professors, neither of which applied to him or his current portfolio. I felt my own pride and self-defense welling up inside me, though of course no one knew but me. I thought to myself, *I could be doing a much better job on that topic. I know those same leaders. Why wasn't I asked to participate in that panel? Certainly I represent a much larger and more prestigious seminary than that person. I've even written about that subject matter.* These were the thoughts going through my mind as I sat there with a holy smile on my face. Of course no one could perceive my inner thoughts or the growing angst in my heart.

And then the wretched reprobate in me emerged. I sat back in my chair, folded my arms, scowled a bit, and simply chose to tune out the speakers up front—until one of my friends, who was sitting behind me, leaned forward and whispered in my ear, "Feeling a bit out of this discussion, man? You could be up there, right?" He said this with sarcastic flair. I was immediately stunned by what he had observed. Was he reading my mind? I was instantly humiliated by the thought of what he must have perceived in my heart.

I turned around and said something snarky back to him (hoping he was oblivious to what was really going on in my heart and mind) and then sat up tall to listen attentively and present myself in a more mature manner. But my friend had no idea what kind of gift he had given to me at that moment. My heart was pierced with sadness and guilt. I immediately prayed a prayer of forgiveness. My pride was so palpable to me, but thankfully for the grace and mercy of God, no one else seemed to notice (of course now you'll remind me of this the next time we're together!).

In our world today, within the Christian community and, yes, even among those of us in the spiritual formation movement, there exists a hero mentality toward noted authors and speakers, driven by those who market both products and personalities. Is it any wonder, therefore, that pride would ultimately seep into the heart of those who are placed on such pedestals? Or into the heart of any number of us wanna-be celebrities?

Having worked for several years for an organization that ran major events, and hosting over thirty such events as leader of that organization, I've seen how pride can emerge and run rampant among big-name personalities (and those who host them). These events welcomed from one thousand to more than ten thousand attendants. On the positive side, they were amazing experiences for the body of Christ. The worship, instruction, networking, resourcing and, most important, the life change that occurred in those settings was nothing short of remarkable, even miraculous at times. I look back with fond recollection to the many years we would gather for those amazingly unique experiences. They marked all of us in deeply profound ways.

But during those events we hosted speakers that flew to the venue in private jets. We agreed to put speakers up in particular hotels and suites that exceeded the budget. We complied with requests for specific dining times and expensive menu requests, and even accommodated large room-service fees to keep said speakers from eating in the public restaurants. We even kept certain notables out of public elevators so they didn't have to deal with attendees gawking at them, asking them off-the-cuff questions or distracting them from their preparation. We saw firsthand what "handlers" did for speakers and received all sorts of demands from the speakers' agents.

Why did we do so? First and foremost because of our own pride, truth be told (as well as the perceived pride of our speakers, musicians, actors and emcees). We were building up our organization, and we had our own goals for growing bigger and becoming better known. We had huge financial demands placed on us, many of which were self- and/or team-imposed, I might add. When you're in the big-event business you begin to think you're pretty special too.

We were negotiating large contracts with big-ticket international hotels, city-owned convention centers and vast exhibit halls, and with vendors who placed chairs on floors, lights in ceilings, security at doorways, signage over escalators, food onto reception tables, balloons suspended from rafters, and on and on. We were interviewed by the media, followed by those who admired our capabilities, and appreciated by those in attendance each year. It was fun, energizing, creative, and filled with adrenaline and joy. And, it was exhausting, competitive and had the capability of puffing one up with the addicting air of self-righteous pride.

Pride comes in all different shapes, sizes and forms and emerges out of a heart that's subtly or overtly lured toward pride and his difficult-to-handle cousin greed. When pride seeps into the pores of a leader's heart, it's nearly impossible to expunge without the grace and mercy of God. Tight-fisted greed wants more and more for self and isn't easily satisfied. The grip of pride and greed runs a leader ragged and tends to ripple outward to all who follow that person. Having identified my own propensity in this regard and been humbled by its reality in my own heart, I've seen the damage it causes within and around a prideful leader. It's not a pretty face to see in one's mirror for sure.

LOVE IS NOT PROUD

Before his conversion, the apostle Paul was well known for his pride. He was an outspoken hater of Christians and the community they represented. He "[breathed] out murderous threats against the Lord's disciples" (Acts 9:1). He called himself a leader who "persecuted the church of God and tried to destroy it" (Galatians 1:13). He was zealous to uphold the traditions of his forefathers, and he was disgusted by the growth of the Christ-following movement that had emerged in his midst. He sought out any man or woman who associated with the Way (of Jesus) in order to take them down as prisoners to Jerusalem.

But God captured his heart dramatically on the road to Damascus (Acts 9) when a light from heaven flashed around him and he fell to the ground and heard, "Saul, Saul, why do you persecute me?" (v. 4). When he realized that the one behind the voice was Jesus, he was struck blind for three days and did not eat or drink anything. As Ananias approached him on Straight Street and laid his hands on Saul, his sight was restored and he was filled with the Holy Spirit. A dramatic conversion occurred in Saul/Paul's heart. With his baptism to enlighten his soul and food to strengthen his body, the apostle was set free from his prideful ways into a new way of living for God, preaching a new gospel of love.

Paul was now abandoned to serve others in Jesus' name. His pride was severed by the light of truth and grace. His life was spared by the generous hand of God. His suffering would continue, but now for a cause much larger than himself. Paul would lead a speaking circuit throughout the land of the Gentiles, in front of their kings and among the people of Israel. There would be no special privileges for him, no handlers to make sure he was well rested and fed. Wherever Paul showed up, a riot and a revolution ensued. This is in sharp contrast to many famous personalities of our day who require tea and crumpets to soothe them for their task at hand while their listeners have their ears tickled about how to enhance their lifestyle.

Each of Paul's missionary journeys proved to the watching world that this grand personality in their midst was on a huge mission: proclaiming the gospel of Jesus Christ to his generation. So when he speaks firmly to the Corinthian church about the need for them to learn how to supremely love—over all other options—he does so within their context of brokenness and suffering. Out of weakness God's strength would emerge, over and over again. Paul's invitation to the Corinthians was very simple: "open wide your hearts" (2 Corinthians 6:13).

Why was this appeal so robust? Because of Paul's perseverance every step of the way and his willingness to serve the Corinthians

> in great endurance; in troubles, hardships and distresses; in beatings, imprisonments and riots; in hard work, sleepless nights and hunger; in purity, understanding, patience and kindness; in the Holy Spirit and in sincere love; in truthful speech and in the power of God; with weapons of righteousness in the right hand and in the left; through glory and dishonor, bad report and good report; genuine, yet regarded as imposters; known, yet regarded as unknown; dying and yet we live on; beaten, and yet not killed; sorrowful, yet always rejoicing; poor, yet making many rich; having nothing, and yet possessing everything. (2 Corinthians 6:4-10)

Paul was an amazing man of God. His prideful zeal *against* Christ was transformed into righteous zeal *for* Christ. He was emboldened with power to break strongholds that false prophets had planted in people's minds and hearts. He was strident for the cause of Christ not out of fear or prideful ambition but for the gospel to be advanced in his generation. Paul had every reason to boast. He was a Hebrew, an Israelite, a descendant of

Abraham. But most important, he was a servant of God, and he was willing to pay the price required of that:

> I am more. I have worked much harder, been in prison more frequently, been flogged more severely, and been exposed to death again and again. Five times I received from the Jews the forty lashes minus one. Three times I was beaten with rods, once I was stoned, three times I was shipwrecked. I spent a night and a day in the open sea, I have been constantly on the move. I have been in danger from rivers, in danger from bandits, in danger from my own countrymen, in danger from Gentiles; in danger in the city, in danger in the country, in danger at sea; and in danger from false brothers. I have labored and toiled and have often gone without sleep; I have known hunger and thirst and have often gone without food; I have been cold and naked. Besides everything else, I face daily the pressure of my concern for all the churches. (2 Corinthians 11:23-28)

His previous pride was broken open, and love was set free.

For Paul to say so plainly "love isn't proud" is to say "love is willing to pay the price of every possible brow-beating action of humility and brokenness if it means you will finally say yes to my simple request: open wide your heart" (my translation). Paul meant what he said and said what he meant. He didn't mince words or soften the message. He was passionate about one thing: that people open wide their heart and receive the love of Christ. And in loving Christ, for Christ's sake, love one another—and make sure to love without pride.

He was not only willing to suffer greatly to get his point across to his followers, he even endured a "thorn in his flesh"—a messenger from Satan to torment him. Yet God reminded him of one central and all-important truth: "'My grace is sufficient for you, for my power is made perfect in weakness.' . . . For when I am weak, then I am strong" (2 Corinthians 12: 9-10). The life of the amazing apostle Paul consisted of finding strength in weakness over and over again.

INVITATION TO GENEROUS HUMILITY

Paul's love for each church he planted and the way it's reflected in generous humility (the opposite of pride and greed) requires leadership that's upside down and contradictory to what our culture espouses today. To follow his example will mean taking bold steps to combat the desire to be first of the class, ahead of all others and given special treatment. Are you willing to take the risk of exposing your own pride, identifying pride in and among your faith communities (local church, specialized ministry, small group, circle of friends, etc.), and talking more freely about the net negative effects of the pride-filled cult of personality we've created today?

If so, then we will need to begin with ourselves. We must seriously and prayerfully embrace humility and generosity as attributes of leadership and of love. As leaders we must model both qualities in our personal and professional life, expressing a love that isn't proud to all who cross our path. This will require a radical transformation of our mind and heart to make them receptive to the planting of seeds that grow the fruit of God's Spirit known as generous humility.

What does generous humility look like? Those who have written about the subject don't necessarily acknowledge it in themselves, but they have identified what the attribute looks like in the heart and life of another. One person who has written about the topic is Saint Benedict, who in the mid-sixth century crafted a "Ladder of Humility" with twelve rungs that lead upward to the goal. He acknowledged that the road to humility is a hard one and is rarely self-guided. It's a road that has been trampled on by others, one where the base is nothing more grandiose than humus, the dirt that encompasses earth and something we simply take for granted.

Benedict's guide leads one upward to the pinnacle of humility, which is counterintuitive to the more conceivable descent toward humility, as described by Bernard of Clairvaux several centuries later. However, the point Benedict (as well as Bernard) is making through the steps toward humility is that a person's self-centered and prideful character is peeled away one layer at a time. This is the process that leads to humility, a movement inward toward further self-effacement, modesty and meekness, which results in the purest possible human love.

In Benedict's treatise on humility (found in chapter seven of his *Rule of Life*, which is readily available and which I recommend to all serious leaders), he moves from a more generalized effort to live a good, moral, upright life. From there, the path to humility includes the concerted work of self-renunciation, and then further into submission to Christ, with endurance and patience, that leads to radical self-honesty and a deeper awareness of one's sinfulness. The more one avoids individualistic and attention-seeking behavior and instead cultivates a listening heart and practices the disciplines of silence, solitude and self-reflection, the more humility is attained. The integration of humility into our heart and life is what leads to ongoing transformation of the heart to love genuinely and more fully.

There are four key terms that emerge from the Ladder of Humility and speak to the ways in which leaders are to love others as they love themselves. If pride is central in our heart, then we will not bear fruit that lasts. If merely considered intellectually or interactively, but are not grounded biblically or experientially, then each term will be lost in translation.

- *Abandonment*: letting go of that which we consider necessary in order to live satisfying and fulfilled lives, including the relationships, possessions, power and pride, as well as activities, attitudes and achievements that we have come to believe define us as people. Can you let them go or, at minimum, hold them more loosely?

- *Contentment*: learning the secret of contentment, as the apostle Paul wrote from his prison cell to the church in Philippi, so that no matter what circumstances or conditions you may find yourself in, an attitude of joyful contentment will prevail. Will you pursue this life-changing posture of heart, mind and will?

- *Integration*: discovering the myriad ways a humble heart should infiltrate each and every aspect of our lives. Our words and deeds, in every setting and in all circumstances, need to be permeated by generous humility. Are you willing to look carefully and prayerfully into the mirror of your heart and seek thoughtful ways of integration?

- *Transformation*: realizing that in order for generous humility to stick long term, it must be allowed to settle deeply in the heart and slowly transform your idea of a desirable life. Authentic transformation happens over time and goes deep, allowing us to generously love and serve others out of a changed heart. Will you abandon any of your identified self-centered ways of living and invite God's Spirit to replace them with generous humility?

Are you so inclined to answer with an enthusiastic yes the invitation to "open wide your heart" to Jesus? If so, the transformed life you live will bring a smile to God's face, filled with love and affection for the renewed you.

Spiritual Leadership Audit

Redeeming Your Pride

When leading others, humility is appreciated far more than anything that smacks of pride. However, our pride is often evoked by our fears: we fear not being recognized or appreciated or even noticed. When this happens, pride comes shouting out from within so that we are in control of what we offer of ourselves to all who cross our pathway. Consider instead how your heart longs for more humble postures of openness and receptivity. Like the soil of the earth, so the soil of your heart desires the seed of loving humility. When the rough edges of your pride are sanded down to a smooth and softer touch, you become a much more delightful person to accompany in life and service to others. As you consider the following exercises of reflection, may they become your soul's most productive moments for the redemption of your pride and the restoration of the sweet aroma of Christlike humility re-created from deep within.

Confess your brokenness: Naming your brokenness and owning it as a present reality.

- In what way(s) have you found yourself prideful, or experienced pridefulness from another, most recently?

- Consider prayerfully the details of this experience and recount them here.

Rest and trust in God's abiding presence and peace: Seeking God's generous humility to be revealed and released from within your soul.

- *Hopeful in Scripture*: Read John 13:1-7 and Philippians 2:5-8. Consider the ways in which Jesus reflected generous humility in his service, relationships, death and resurrection.

- *Faithful in prayer*: Jesus said, "Learn from me, for I am gentle and humble in heart" (Matthew 11:29). Ask Jesus in prayer how you can learn from him how to become more meek and humble of heart. Spend time listening attentively to his gentle invitations.

- *Thankful in reflection*: Recall the time most recently when you were the recipient of generous humility on the part of another. Review your key relationships and note the people in your life whom you consider most generous and humble. What are their traits or lifestyle choices that you most desire to emulate?

Invite God to redeem your brokenness: Restoring God's loving humility in you. Recall the story of King David's brokenness and his subsequent prayer in Psalm 51, which was written after being lovingly confronted by Nathan. Ask God to create in you a pure heart and renew a right spirit toward yourself and others.

- Identify where in your heart, head and hands you remain closed up and protective.

- If prideful, tight-fisted greed resides in your heart today, invite the Spirit of God to instead plant an openhanded and generous humility into your heart, expressed outward toward all you are called to serve today.

- Look at your own open hands and ask God to keep them open to receive and give in your relationship with the Lord, with others and even with yourself. Consider maintaining an openhanded posture each new day, and watch how your heart remains supple to the fresh movements of God's Spirit in, through and around you.

five

The Maddening Manipulation of Self and Others

Love is not rude

"OH MY GOODNESS, HAVE YOU EVER experienced a church meeting of all church meetings?" This was the opening query from Fred, a church consultant, who shared the following amazing story with me. As he spoke, all I could do was shake my head in disbelief.

Fred had never before seen what transpired one autumn evening when he was asked to moderate a congregational meeting for a church in conflict. The senior pastor had recently resigned and taken several dozen parishioners with him to plant a new church a few miles away. His exit wasn't pretty. The church family was gathering to process all of this and make some decisions about how best to move forward.

The now-former pastor's influence had slowly over time caused a huge rift in the church. There were those who thought very highly of his academic acumen and provocative preaching. But there was an equal number who felt he was distancing himself from the real needs of people and hurting many by the heavy-handed misuse of his self-projected and authoritative power. When he first came to the congregation a vast majority of parishioners received him with lofty expectations. After all, he was the fourth pastor to enter this church since the much-beloved founding pastor had left nearly twelve years earlier. His path was wide open for exploration and expansion. Everyone was optimistic and ready for the change.

But slowly, over the few years he was there, the chasm began to grow. His strongest advocates were those who were the most conservative ones in the congregation. They affirmed his leadership and defended his tactics every step of the way, even when his maneuvers became offensive and cold-hearted. Why? Because he was a man of the Word with solid theology and very firm convictions. Therefore he thought he had the right to be a bit brash and overbearing. On the other side of the aisle, literally and figuratively, were those who didn't appreciate his lack of emotion in the pulpit (juxtaposed to his theological passions) and his perceived hardhearted coldness toward many in the pew.

So when it came time for the infamous congregational meeting, the great divide was fully exposed. Those in defense of the former pastor spoke up doggedly and determinedly. They were strong in their resolve and loud in their demeanor. They were demanding and came with a fighting spirit, ready to win any argument and trump any disagreement. They made their presence known through their verbal projections from the strategically placed microphones and in their antics among the congregation. Some were even using their smartphones to videotape comments from the "other side," while others simply talked over those who were meeker in their presentation, even though Fred repeatedly asked them not to do so.

What emerged throughout the three-hour gathering was incredible to observe. Fred had never seen such hurtful antics in church life before. He was there to supposedly moderate the meeting as an objective outsider, but he too received their brutal attacks. In fact, one young man, Tim, stood to make a comment from his seat rather than standing behind a microphone, and when Fred reminded him of the meeting protocol, he gave Fred an earful. Tim's concluding statement to Fred was stunning: "You have no voice in this meeting. When you are ready to leave we will gladly show you the door and usher you out to your car," and then proceeded to deliver his prepared statement. Fred was dumbfounded and appalled.

What began as a congregational meeting led off by a few worship songs and prayers quickly drifted into an irrational and out of control secular meeting. The first to make a statement was a man who had resigned as an elder immediately after the pastor resigned. He came to the pulpit to read his statement, which was more akin to an accusation leveled against the remaining elders. He had already left the church with the former pastor, but felt compelled to return to this meeting and issue his remarks. This was followed by one nasty statement after another, mostly against those who had supposedly "run the pastor out of the pulpit" and taken over the church for a litany of assumed selfish reasons.

Whenever someone stepped cautiously to the microphone to share tearfully how the pastor had hurt them or members of their family, Fred could feel the vitriol in the room. Within a few moments there were put-downs leveled against those who emotionally shared their concerns. This went on, back and forth, for nearly two hours, one person after another, teeter-tottering from people in support of the former pastor to those who had been hurt by him. There simply didn't seem to be anyone present with an objective point of view. The two sides were at odds with one another, and despite efforts from Fred and the existing elders to call for decency or kindness, the negativity and counter-productivity went on relentlessly.

One attempt at peace making came from a middle-aged woman, Tammy, who spoke up two hours into the meeting. She made some rather gentle suggestions about how to seek resolution, and with a very humble heart. This evoked even more combative responses and resulted in those who had earlier excused themselves to the vestibule to conspire together coming back into the sanctuary for additional rebuttal. They sought to quiet her down but were unsuccessful in their attempt. She simply kept standing, never leaving her place at the microphone, and lovingly confronted those who were trying to shut her down. Her humility was abundant, and her grace silenced the opposition, as several simply left the meeting in exasperation.

Tammy's persistent grace cleared the room of the vitriol, and her loving spirit broke the ice. Tim, who had previously ripped into Fred, stood up and apologized publicly for his outburst. He and Tammy became the catalysts for restrained speech and restored order for the rest of the meeting. What could have been disastrous ended up being restorative. With the most vehement people now gone from the meeting, some prayerful attempts to put pieces back together began to unfold.

When the existing elder chair resumed control of the meeting, he very humbly shared what the remaining elder team was in the process of doing to help bring reconciliation and restoration back to the church. By this time, with most of the verbal naysayers gone, the mood in the room had tempered significantly, and those who endured were ready to consider a direction for the days ahead. A few helpful suggestions were aired after the chair shared the elders' ideas, and finally the meeting was adjourned in prayer and peace.

Fred told me how, as he drove home that night, he grieved for this congregation. He prayed that God's hand of loving mercy would remain over each and every person who had gathered. He recalled the various comments that were shared and considered the faces of the ones who were bold enough to stand up against the bullies in the room. And he remembered afresh how Jesus dealt with people in his life who had spoken up harshly against him, tried to belittle his tender meekness, attempted to contradict his convictions or sought ways to undermine his authority.

And, Fred humbly thought, only by the grace of God was he not also at times the rudest one in the room.

Love Is Not Rude

One thing is pretty consistently true about every rude person: they must set the agenda. They must be in control. The twentieth-century American social philosopher Eric Hoffer once said, "Rudeness is the weak man's imitation of strength"; I would modify this to read "Rudeness is the self-protected and highly manipulative person's projection of power." Rudeness is based in the need to be in control, to be right, to be strong in what the world says strength looks like: power over others. To be powerful *over* another doesn't necessarily mean strength, for strength as we've been unpacking it in this book can also be shown more effectively through weakness and humility.

Rudeness is conveyed in various ways. It can appear through a foul mouth or unsuitable speech. It can be expressed through an inappropriate use of one's middle finger and the dominance this evokes. It can be communicated by way of physical roughness or pushiness. It can overwhelm another by showing little concern or regard for that person's personal property or space. It can disturb the mind, destroy the heart or dismantle the morals of others. In essence, a rudeness of personhood is abuse of power by seeking outright control and manipulation.

When Paul writes "love isn't rude" he's saying, "love doesn't abuse power." He's saying, "love isn't manipulative," and "love isn't controlling." To the Corinthians, he's in essence saying, "I'm calling you to the most excellent way to lead and serve others in Jesus' name, and it's all about love. And this love that I'm inviting you to embrace isn't one that manipulates and then expresses that control in a rude or obnoxious way. Therefore, stop always having to set the agenda!"

Paul would later write to the Galatians about what it means to be filled with the Spirit. The fruit, or evidence of that kind of life, is made manifest in love, joy, peace, patience, kindness, goodness, faithfulness, gentleness and self-control. When this kind of life emerges from the Christ-following, Spirit-empowered person, the way in which they relate to one another isn't rude. Instead, it's gracious and loving, not with a firm hand or a clenched fist, but with an openly generous hand, a willing heart and a spiritual mind.

When he began his letter to the Corinthians, Paul spoke immediately into the divisions in the church. His appeal to them was that they be united in mind and thought. To not let divisions separate them or, through human wisdom, to overpower one another. Then he sets out how this is to come about: by being united in the wisdom of Christ and the power of God. This is in contrast to the Jews demanding miraculous signs and Greeks looking for worldly wisdom.

Paul's call to the Corinthians was to preach Christ crucified, which would be a stumbling block to the Jews who were in search of signs, and foolishness to the Greeks looking for worldly wisdom. "For the foolishness of God is wiser than man's wisdom, and the weakness of God is stronger than man's strength"

(1 Corinthians 1:25). He reminds them of their respective starting places when they were called to faith: "Not many of you were
wise by human standards; not many were influential; not many
were of noble birth. But God chose the foolish things of the
world to shame the wise; God chose the weak things of the world
to shame the strong. He chose the lowly things of this world and
the despised things—and the things that are not—to nullify the
things that are, so that no one may boast before him" (1 Corinthians 1:26-29). It is because of Christ that righteousness, holiness and redemption are received, not one's human eloquence
or superior speech, which can so rudely dominate others and
create division and fear.

Paul is reminding the Corinthians that it was only by a demonstration of the Spirit's power that they might learn to rest on
God's power for themselves. It was not because they were so
humanly wise, influential or had come from a noble birth. He
continues in chapter 2 to describe the wisdom that comes from
the Spirit; secret wisdom that's hidden from this world so that
God's glory is revealed through its uniqueness. This is not what
the world or the rulers of this age understand as power or might;
it's only fully regarded as such by those who trust in the Spirit.

Then in chapter 3 he goes back to the issue of divisions once
again and declares with even more boldness that there are two
ways to deal with divisions: one is spiritual, and the other is
worldly. Paul reminds them that he could only give them milk
as mere infants in Christ, not solid food, which is for the more
spiritually mature. Why? Because they were still worldly, quarreling among themselves, acting immaturely just like others in
their secular city. The more mature response of love required a
deeper awareness of the firm foundation of Jesus Christ, which
had already been laid for them. Their rudeness toward one
another was evidence of their ongoing immaturity.

He warns them about building on a foundation firmly established for them. "If any man builds on this foundation using gold,
silver, costly stones, wood, hay or straw, his work will be shown
for what it is, because the Day will bring it to light. It will be
revealed with fire, and the fire will test the quality of each man's
work" (1 Corinthians 3:12-13). Instead, Paul urges them to build
their lives around the reality that they are God's temple, a sacred
place to reside, and it's the Spirit who resides within them. Don't
be rude or crafty about any of this, as if to be worldly leaders, he
says; instead, be filled up with the Spirit, even when it appears
as foolishness to others. In other words, abusing power and
always setting the agenda without relying on the Spirit smacks
of the world's form of leading others. Instead, be wise, strong
and blessed in Christ.

Paul continues this plea in chapter 4 with a strong appeal to
the leaders of the Corinthian church as apostles of Christ: avoid
pride and arrogance, and receive instead the power that comes
from the Spirit. "Some of you have become arrogant. . . . I will
find out not only how these arrogant people are talking, but
what power they have. For the kingdom of God is not a matter
of talk but of power. What do you prefer? Shall I come to you
with a whip, or in love and with a gentle spirit?" (1 Corinthians
4:18-21). From this place he then speaks to one major issue at a
time, from expelling the immoral brother to lawsuits, sexual
immorality, marriage, idolatry and worship (chapters 5–11) and
comes back once again to unity and oneness (chapter 12).

When Paul says love isn't rude, he's inviting his listeners to
consider the opposite of rudeness, which ultimately breaks
down divisions in the church and builds unity among the believers. That kind of expression toward others looks more like
respect, kindness, gentleness, politeness and graciousness.
Where does such a heart come from? It is impossible to

manufacture in the strength of our humanity. It only emerges from a reflective, contemplative, openhanded and Spirit-controlled life. Sound impossible? Only if considered from a human perspective. It is fully possible, however, in the Spirit.

INVITATION TO SELF-REFLECTION AND SPIRIT-CONTROL

If we are ever to have such a reflective, contemplative, open-handed and Spirit-controlled life, then we must begin by admitting when the opposite exists in our heart. We must learn to acknowledge when and how and under what conditions we find ourselves needing to set the agenda, either forcefully or passively. None of us like to be manipulated, taken advantage of, lied to, talked over or ignored by another. Neither do we appreciate having to listen to the craftiness and cunningness of deceit that comes from those who are twisting or spinning the story to get their point across. Worse yet is when we find ourselves doing those exact things!

Can you recall times in your life when you've been rude and have abused your power over others? When you've needed to set the agenda for another either forcefully with words or actions, or passively via subtle, coy, subversive or passive-aggressive means? The bottom line here is that when we are rude toward another and seek to lord it over them by needing to be the one setting the agenda or outcome, we are being manipulative.

I will never forget confessing to my spiritual director the trouble I was having with my wife, one of my children and one of my coworkers. Each story had a common thread running through it: my need to influence another toward my stated agenda. I had opinions about each person expressed, of course, as concerns, but each person had not taken me up on my suggestions. Instead, each of them had done the exact opposite of the wise insight I offered to them. All of them had made up their own minds and determined their own course of action. And none of their decisions pleased me. I was agitated, aggravated and beside myself with disappointment. It was a dark moment for me.

My spiritual director looked at me and said very matter-of-factly, "Steve, if you continue to be manipulative toward those you love and serve, you will continue to be disappointed. Unless you learn to be more reflective and contemplative in your prayers for them and your actions and words toward them, you will simply continue to be manipulative. What's your choice?"

Afterward, I repeated this phrase over and over and over again: "Unless I learn to be more contemplative, I will continue to be manipulative . . . unless I learn to be more prayerfully reflective, I will continue to be manipulative." There was so much truth to that insight I needed to receive and ponder deeply. Frankly, those simple phrases have changed my life.

- For those who choose to be rude and set the agenda for others, there is a corresponding need to manage the approach and outcomes. Instead of managing, we need to learn to let it go and trust God for his will at all times.

- For those who continue to be manipulative toward others in their life and think they have the best ideas for others' lifestyle decisions, there is a clarion call to change. Instead of manipulating, reflectively consider and contemplatively pray for those we are seeking to control and trust God for his will at all times.

- For those who keep an eye on others and monitor their every move, it's time to look to God and ask the Spirit to help you focus elsewhere. Instead of continuous monitoring of every aspect of this person's life or situation, simply pray for them and trust God for his will at all times.

- For those who feel it's their calling in life to manage and maintain the necessary focus on the process and end result, it's best to see the big picture and the long view. Instead of managing, it's far better to move on to love and serve others in Jesus' name, and trust God for his will at all times.

At all times and at all costs, choosing a more reflective, contemplative, openhanded and Spirit-controlled life is the best way to go.

Imagine how the opening story of the church meeting would have unfolded if it had been approached in this regard. The time together would have looked completely different. The rude leader who imposed his agenda up front would have rewritten his remarks to be more affirming of all concerned. The persons who came with an express desire to loudly out-shout and embarrass others would instead have been gentle of voice and heart and would not have condemned or shamed anyone for any reason. The person who stood up to suggest the former pastor come back to share his perspective would have received a more loving hearing. The young man Tim would have been grateful for the presence of an objective presence moderating the meeting. There would have been no conversations behind the scenes or out in the vestibule. The opening worship and prayer time would have lingered much longer. The existing elder team would have been applauded for their efforts and prayed over for wisdom in leading them in the days ahead. The division that existed before and during the meeting would have been confessed earlier, the brokenness of the people exposed, and a heartfelt reconciliation could have occurred with all the members present. That would have been a more excellent way.

Instead, many of the members chose their own worldly way. They let other voices speak into and about their hurt and negatively affect their heart. They used their own voices in words, tone and body language that were hurtful and offensive to their extended church family. They even showed actions that expressed rudeness and discourteousness to one another. They very simply forgot what Paul wrote to the divided church in Corinth, and to each one of them today: love is never rude.

May the church at large become more of a place of grace than one where rudeness is allowed to occur unbridled and unchecked. Love simply has no room for rudeness.

Spiritual Leadership Audit

Restoring Your Self-Reflection and Spirit-Control

Rudeness is everywhere today—in relationships, politics, education and even religion. Our generation is so evocative of the time when Corinth was a center of cultural expressions that were in direct opposition to the way Christ walked this earth and invited his disciples to live. When others were rude to Jesus, his responses were always reflective and thoughtful. His use of questions and parables to bring out truths were invitational to his hearers. In like fashion, the following reflection suggestions are intended to evoke a story, memory or metaphor in your personal journey. Hopefully these reflections will invite you to consider afresh what your life would be like if rudeness were expunged from your heart and replaced instead by the love of God. Allow the Holy Spirit to prompt you to consider that which matters most in this regard.

Confess your brokenness: Naming your brokenness and owning it as a present reality.

- In what way(s) have you found yourself rude and manipulative, or experienced rudeness or manipulation from another, most recently?

- Consider prayerfully the details of this experience and recount them here.

Rest and trust in God's abiding presence and peace: Seeking God's Spirit-control to be revealed and released from within your soul.

- *Hopeful in Scripture*: Read 1 Corinthians 13:11 several times: "When I was a child, I talked like a child, I thought like a child, I reasoned like a child. When I became a man, I put childish ways behind me." In what ways is rudeness immature?

- *Faithful in prayer*: Sit prayerfully with the question, "When I am rude, what childish or childlike need is being most vividly expressed?"

- *Thankful in reflection*: Rudeness often goes undetected by the perpetrator of rudeness . . . and that includes you and me. When you do see rudeness in your attitude, actions or words, very simply say, "Isn't that interesting" and then reflect on what's being provoked in you that's prompting a rude response. Attend carefully to what you notice and jot it down. Is there a prayer formulating in your heart to offer in response?

Invite God to redeem your brokenness: Restoring God's loving Spirit-control in you. Embrace your rude and self-directed ways, and ask the Spirit to restore self-control, which leads to greater obedience to God's will and ways.

- Memorize the phrase "Isn't that interesting," so that during times when you are rude toward others you can repeat this phrase to yourself and make it a prayer to the Lord. It's times like these when you need God's empowering presence instead of your own human desire for a rude or inappropriate response. This will aid your growth in self-reflection and prayerful contemplation of your attitudes and actions toward others, and will open up a more mindful, thoughtful response.

- Give voice to any way that your rudeness may have hurt another. Note the importance of these simple conflict-resolving and relationally life-giving phrases "I'm sorry," "I was wrong," "Please forgive me," and "I love you." Do any or all of these need to be voiced to another in your sphere of influence today?

- If rudeness exists among your ministry or within your team, consider how best to eradicate it from everyone's shared experience. Talk candidly about this with all who share in leadership, and if necessary, remain open to inviting an outside resource to come into your setting and advise you in how best to replace immature rudeness with the refreshing maturity of God's love.

- six -

Is an Independent Spirit
in Your Veins and Arteries?

Love is not self-seeking

WHEN AMANDA AND GREG WERE first married, Amanda was a self-professed driven woman on a mission. She wasn't pushy toward others but was internally focused on becoming a successful business professional. And, in the early 1990s she was on the front end of the technology bubble in the Canadian firm where she landed her first job. Fresh out of college and hoping to complete her master's degree with the help of her employer, Amanda had a bright and promising future. Greg was very proud of his ambitious wife, as he too was destined for greatness in his vocation as a rising star in the finance industry.

Raised in a family where her parents poured courage into her heart and mind from early childhood, Amanda was exposed to a world of endless opportunities. They lived in an affluent suburb of Toronto, and as a teenager she excelled in almost everything she participated in. She was a scholar in the classroom, an athlete on the field, and popular among her peers. She had a sweet disposition, not at all pretentious or arrogant about how blessed she was in most areas of life. She simply enjoyed the challenges and privileges afforded her with each new day.

She and Greg met one another in their first semester of college. They attended a lot of business classes together and made the most of those formative years. Greg and Amanda dated throughout their four years at the university and were one of those near-perfect couples, with virtually everything going their way. And, remarkably, they were surrounded by a sea of friends who were peers in most areas of their personal lives: successful, hard working, fun loving and even godly. They enjoyed those years tremendously.

One of the priorities they both shared was being involved in the student Christian fellowship on campus. They were both in a small group, attended the weekly gatherings and tried to attend at least one retreat each year. So when Greg proposed to Amanda, they were committed to Christ and a Christ-centered marriage. They were married within two months of graduation. Their wedding ceremony was wonderful, and all in attendance blessed the celebration of their oneness in marriage.

For the first couple years, Greg and Amanda enjoyed the fullness of their lives. They rented a trendy apartment just outside the city and quickly established a healthy routine together. At their two-year anniversary, Amanda pronounced that she was pregnant. Their families were thrilled with the news and excited about their first grandchild.

What no one expected was Amanda's decision to stop working after the baby arrived. Overnight she gave up her ambition to make it big in the technology industry. Her maternal instincts emerged fully, and all she wanted was to be a mom. She quit her job and stayed home with her children, raising three daughters over the next twenty years. She had no regrets whatsoever and felt it was the best decision of her life. In time, everyone agreed.

So, when in 2010 the last of their three daughters entered high school, Amanda announced to Greg that she wanted to go back to work. There was an opportunity in their local church for an executive director position, overseeing the administrative and financial functions of the church. She would be working directly for the senior pastor, a friend of the family and someone she highly respected. Greg was open to the idea, so she applied and was offered the job.

Amanda's drivenness as a worker quickly reemerged after being dormant for nearly two decades. She loved her new job and felt it would fit well into their family system at this stage of life. What no one realized at the time is how focused she would be on becoming a success—all by herself.

At first everything was going smoothly. She got to know the team already in place in this large church and quickly earned their respect. She had six people in the office she supervised on a daily basis and another six pastoral staff members she resourced as a peer on the organizational chart. She had lay committees to work with and a handful of key leaders to report to from the board. She seemed to relate well with everyone, but over time she began to take on projects in isolation and without any communication with others. She jumped head first into the deep waters of ministry and accomplished a lot in a short period of time, but always alone and in a very driven way.

All of this came to light when the board asked her for an update on the new software system recently installed. She gave a report of the work she had done and all appeared smooth at the time. But the real story emerging behind the scenes was that she had made a unilateral decision to abandon the system the team had decided to purchase. Instead, she did some of her own research and chose another system. She installed it during off hours with the help of outside services that came with a hefty price tag. However, the system failed; it was not properly installed, and it was poorly designed. She had been out of the world of technology for so long, and her choice of a system proved disastrous. All the financial and personal data of the church membership was lost. No back-ups were in place. The system failed. The church came to a standstill in every regard. There was no simple or inexpensive way to recover the years of work lost. And Amanda pointed fingers and blamed everyone possible, not taking the responsibility she most deserved. Eventually everything came to light, and she was immediately fired.

For months this deeply affected Amanda, and she refused to go to church or seek help. She was humiliated beyond comprehension and had a difficult time finding her way out of this darkness. She balked at the idea of confessing her wrongdoing and doing the hard work of reconciliation and restoration, revealing her independent spirit. This resistance lasted for nearly eleven months, when one day the pastor showed up at her doorstep unannounced. When she opened the door and saw his face, she quickly shut the door. But he put his foot in the way and pleaded with her to let him come inside. Greg was with him, and when together they entered the vestibule of their home, Amanda wept. Her pent-up anguish came pouring out, and she apologized profusely for making such a mess for the church, offering to come and repent to the team and even suggesting she come back on staff without pay as recompense for her actions.

None of her ideas were acted on that day. But over time she was able to return to the church with her family. She sought wise counsel from a mentor and a therapist, who helped her understand why she ended up in this predicament. She met with the staff, board and several key lay leaders. She confessed her wrongdoing, especially not consulting with them or working as a team. Her stubborn desire to be successful in their eyes had driven her to distraction. Her failure had come due to her prideful independence. She had learned a significant lesson, which would have positive ripples for years to come. Thankfully, even though she was not hired back on the church staff team, today Amanda is flourishing in a role on a parachurch ministry leadership team where her gifts fit well. She's a part of a large team and values each member with heightened awareness of the need to work together if great things are to be done for the kingdom of God.

LOVE IS NOT SELF-SEEKING

Doing our own thing. Making our own decisions. Setting our own course. Seeking our own acclaim. Taking care of self. Pursuing our own destiny. We each have our own expressions of what it means to be self-seeking. For some, it's demonstrated through examples like Amanda. For others, selfishness comes in different ways. It may be through our work, our play, our vocations or our avocations. It may be seen in our portfolios, our handicaps, our waistlines, our biceps, our mirrors, our wardrobe or our possessions. It may be evident to many, to some or to just a few. No matter how you slice it, we all suffer from this common ill: selfishness. It's in the fiber of our fallen being. And our soul is desperate for it to be redeemed and restored.

When Paul was writing to the Corinthians, all of his teachings were in rebuttal to their propensity to insist on their own way. Therefore, Paul's retort over and over again was for them to not live in the same way as their culture, which was pagan, immoral and filled with debauchery. Each of the issues identified in the first eleven chapters of 1 Corinthians is flipped upside down by Paul, offering the Corinthians a new and liberating way of handling their self-absorbed, divisive, worldly habits.

The apex of the book is chapter 13, when he speaks eloquently of how they are to love in the most excellent way. This is preceded by the latter half of chapter 12, which speaks to their unity as the body of Christ. Seventeen times the apostle Paul uses the word *body* in these eighteen verses. He is using this repetition to highlight an all-important theme: instead of being self-seekers, become others-minded. In the manifestation and outward expression of one's spiritual gifts within the community of faith (1 Corinthians 12:1-11), there is to be unity of the Spirit and oneness in Christ.

This oneness is best exemplified by a unified body. And the apostle takes great pain to describe the essence of that community: a body made up of *many parts*, like a hand, an ear and an eye, that all perform a uniquely *non-competitive* function within the body (vv. 12-17). They are *placed there by God*, just as he wanted them to be (v. 18), they are *interdependently* linked to one another (vv. 20-21), and each has its own *special purpose and priority* in weakness or strength, indispensable presentation and modest treatment (vv. 22-24). All are to show *equal concern* for one another, suffering when another suffers and rejoicing when another is honored (vv. 25-26). Therefore, as each is a member of such a body, Paul implores them to be *fully a part of it*, whether they are an apostle, prophet, teacher, miracle worker, healer, helper, administrator or pray-er (vv. 27-30). No one gift is of greater importance than another. All are needed and affirmed by God and are to be treated equally among his body.

Paul's urging here is reminiscent of his instructions to the Roman church in chapter 12 of that letter, where he calls the people of God to no longer be self-serving, but instead to love one another with sincerity: "Be devoted to one another in brotherly love. Honor one another above yourselves. . . . Share with God's people who are in need. Practice hospitality. Bless those who persecute you; bless and do not curse. Rejoice with those who rejoice; mourn with those who mourn. Live in harmony with one another. . . . Do not repay anyone evil for evil. . . . If it is possible, as far as it depends on you, live at peace with everyone" (Romans 12:10-18). Here Paul offers specific ways to show each other what it means to love in a self-effacing and others-oriented way.

All of Paul's teachings on love come from the example of Jesus, who loved his disciples in the way Paul describes love. This is most specifically noted in Jesus' willingness to wash their feet, the lowliest of servant-like tasks. That act was the full expression of his love for them. And it's to be the same for us. Holding the foot of another and tenderly washing their feet is one of the most humble and intimate expressions of selfless love. Many don't want their feet touched by another, for a myriad of reasons. But even so, it is a deep expression of love unlike many other ways we come alongside others to love and serve them in Jesus' name. To hold the foot of a friend or stranger and to linger in that posture builds unity, community and fellowship like few other expressions. Imagine holding tenderly the foot of your archrival or enemy, never mind your brother, sister or friend. How long would that person stay as an adversary in your heart?

When Paul says to the Corinthians, "love isn't self-seeking," he's reminding them that they live in community with others who are in pursuit of a lifestyle that honors God in every way. A self-seeking love will not help to build unity among the body. Instead, it will continue to divide and disperse people away from one another as they each seek their own interests ahead of others.

There is truly a more excellent way: a love that seeks first the kingdom of God in the hearts and lives of others who share their pathway to an abundant life in Christ. It's not a lonely, independent, self-reliant, self-gratifying journey, but instead is one that pursues the with-God life together, with and for and among the family of God. To restore one's heart, mind and will in this alternative way creates the kind of love and life that honors God and satisfies the soul.

INVITATION TO COMMUNITY

As much as I love people and value community, I often tire from the work of creating and maintaining healthy relationships. It's far easier to be self-seeking in the expression of my love than to be others-motivated. To live independently and consider my needs alone is by far the simplest and cleanest way to live. And it leads to far fewer disappointments and heartaches (unless, of course, my choices negatively impact myself or others). I can see clearly why Paul speaks directly in opposition to being self-seeking, but it doesn't mean I like it. I'm sure you can agree.

Community is messy. It's exhausting, confusing at times and hard to maintain. It's even more challenging to restore. But we are not made to live alone. Instead, we are made for community; I'm sure that's why Paul kept stressing its importance. And our communities look like our marriages, families, churches, neighborhoods, workplaces and cities. We aren't clones of one another, so it's incumbent upon us to get to know one another, deeply and from the heart. To get close to each other requires time and effort, talking and listening, giving and receiving, learning and growing, living and forgiving, encouraging and celebrating. None of this comes naturally to us or easily by osmosis. We have to work at it, strive for it, prioritize it and hold one another accountable for it.

What will it take for us to see life through as others-seeking lovers, learners and leaders? The place to begin is to *embrace our propensity toward an independent spirit.* Owning the reality of your preference for self-seeking is the first admission to acknowledge. Take a look at your current state of soul. Embrace the truth about your inner life. Be willing to go to that quiet place of silence and solitude to wrestle with the reality of your heart and life and the quality (or lack thereof) of your relationships. In the crucible of transformation, silence and solitude is the best venue for discovering the true you.

Invite the Spirit of God to shine a bright light on your personality, your preferences toward selfish gain, and your propensity to care first and foremost for your own well-being. Jot down what you notice, and pray into the truth that's exposed. The best way to unlock your heart and open up yourself to the enlightenment of the Spirit is to prayerfully, reflectively and honestly look in the mirror and own your true self. Then, open up yourself to God, invite him to illumine your heart and mind, and remain pliable to the new and renewing work of his Spirit.

Second, *look around and see who is in your current community*. Assess that reality, for good or for ill, by listing the roles you carry and the relationships that are numbered under each role. For me, the roles of husband, father, child of God, leader, spiritual director, teacher and mentor come quickly to mind. Seven roles, but within each role, except for husband, father and child of God, there are numerous relationships. In my work I oversee two dozen team members, collaborate with a half-dozen board members and foster meaningful connections with several dozen major donors, all under one role: leader.

Therefore, to look realistically at my ministry community, I must consider hundreds of names. But there's no way I can relate to all of them at the same level of intensity. I need to prioritize my relationships within each role and in so doing make sure that the most important people receive my most significant time. Then, learning how best to relate to them when we are together is the fodder for building up each person and becoming the very best I can be for all within my community. Each and every person matters greatly to God and thereby matters significantly to me. So, I need to be sure to give everyone their due in terms of quality and quantity of time. It's not easy to be sure, especially as the numbers of relationships expand and multiply.

Third, we need to begin to *make decisions that will lead to deeper relationships with others* within our various communities. Since community is best defined in the Scriptures through the fifty-plus "one anothers," this is a great place to begin. Learning how to love and serve one another, pray and care for one another, bear the burdens of one another and forgive whatever grievances we have toward one another (just to name a few) is difficult to do on a consistent basis. That's why it's incumbent upon us to prayerfully consider who, what and how to best serve others in a loving way, fulfilling the "one anothers" in a manner pleasing to God.

We are called to lead the way toward the fulfillment of the Great Commandment and the golden rule, all in a manner befitting the one anothers. Perhaps this is the place for you to commence your personal reflections on the state of your relationships and the impact of your community. Loving God with our heart, soul, mind and strength and then loving our neighbors as we love ourselves is the fundamental truth we are to hang our hat on as believers and leaders.

Love is the greatest gift that God gives. Love is also the greatest gift that we can give. And to love as God loves means that we're not to be self-seeking. Instead, we are to love selflessly, generously and with forgiveness. That's only possible in and with God. It's impossible to live this way in our own strength. We need to die to the notion that we can muster up the inner strength to fulfill this mandate on our own and instead open-handedly receive the love of God for ourselves so that we have his love to offer another. The only real corrective to self-seeking is God-seeking. There simply is no other way.

Christian love is not about us but about others. When we put love into practice we are called to follow the example of Jesus, consider the needs and interests of others before our own, and deny our own personal desires in lieu of those we love and serve in Jesus' name. If we keep demanding our own way, trampling on others' rights in order to uphold our own, and insisting on getting what we think we deserve out of life, we will never learn how to be considerate of others. "Look not only to your own interests, but also to the interests of others" (Philippians 2:4)— this command is a simple appeal to the selflessness that comes out of a life fully devoted to Jesus and his amazing example of tireless love.

Spiritual Leadership Audit

Restoring Your Community

When we succumb to self-gratification, self-absorption, self-promotion, self-protection, self-aggrandizement, self-referencing or any other of the myriad ways we self-focus in this self-centered world, we get fixated on ourselves and totally miss others. When we come to believe that if we don't take care of ourselves, no one else will, then we have bought into a lie. We are made for community. We are designed for one another. We are at our best when we align with those of like heart and mind. We thrive when we are loved, known and growing in love for those God has given us to share life. How firm is your foundation of resting assuredly in the awareness of how deeply you are known and loved by God? Out of a growing certainty of being known and loved, how is the Lord inviting you into a lifestyle focused on knowing and loving others in Jesus' name? May the following questions and reflections deepen your affection for Jesus, the lover of your soul, and for his kingdom community.

Confess your brokenness: Naming your brokenness and owning it as a present reality.

- In what way(s) have you found yourself independent and self-seeking, or experienced independence or self-seeking from another, most recently?

- Consider prayerfully the details of this experience and recount them here.

Rest and trust in God's abiding presence and peace: Seeking God's gift of community to be revealed and released from within your soul.

- *Hopeful in Scripture*: Sit with the verse "Do nothing out of selfish ambition or vain conceit, but in humility consider others better than yourselves" (Philippians 2:3). In what ways have you recently acted out of selfish ambition or vain conceit?

- *Faithful in prayer*: Ask the Lord to reveal his invitation to you for a life known for humility of heart rather than the pursuit of a self-seeking heart.

- *Thankful in reflection*: Confess to the Lord the names of those you find it most challenging to love selflessly and considerately. What is it about each of these persons that evokes from within you a response to care for self before serving them in Jesus' name?

Invite God to redeem your brokenness: Restoring God's loving gift of community in you. In his book *Life Together*, Dietrich Bonhoeffer stressed the importance of silence and solitude as a gift for community: "Let him who cannot be alone beware of community. . . . Let him who is not in community beware of being alone. . . . Each by itself has profound perils and pitfalls.

One who wants fellowship without solitude plunges into the void of words and feelings, and the one who seeks solitude without fellowship perishes in the abyss of vanity, self-infatuation and despair."

- Consider the gifts that emerge from the alone space of silence and solitude and jot them down.

- Then recount the gifts that come from a healthy community.

- Notice how the two lists are joined together, and then lean fully into both so that your alone time is enhanced by your community and vice versa.

seven

The Destructive Power of Unbridled Anger

Love is not easily angered

Do you remember the story of the Hatfields and McCoys, the bitterly feuding families of West Virginia (Hatfields) and Kentucky (McCoys) of late-nineteenth-century fame? A "warring faction" indeed, localized alongside the Tug Fork of the Big Sandy River, divided not only by the river but by the economy (wealthy Hatfields and working-class McCoys) and, of course, the war (Hatfields for the Confederacy and McCoys for the Union). Usually on the top of the list of famous family feuds in American history, the Hatfields and McCoys have become synonymous with anger and hatred. With revenge reigning supreme in their hearts toward one another, to this day we associate their family names with words like *meanness, anger* and *division*. Not the keenest of family legacies to be sure.

They were the first names I thought of at a church leadership team meeting I was invited to facilitate. Of the sixteen people around the table that night, more than half of them were from two families in the church. Divided equally, they sat on opposite sides of the large square-table configuration of the four eight-foot tables in the room. There were cousins, aunts, uncles and in-laws all represented that night. No one told me this was the make-up of the group, not even the pastor; it was an insight I had to somehow glean on my own.

I should have known better. I had been working with this church leadership team for about three months when this meeting finally occurred. I had attended an introductory meeting with a majority of the group, where we discussed the process I was prepared to walk them through together. It was a discernment process I was familiar with and had led others through in the past. That earlier meeting had gone quite well, and I was invited to serve the team for the upcoming six-month period of time. They were willing to embrace the topics and experiences together and seemed excited about what they would be learning as a result. We entered an official agreement and set off on our shared expedition.

The first round of meetings was about the spiritual vitality of each individual and of the team collectively. We talked about issues of personal formation, spiritual practices, and ways to include these both in their personal prayer and during their ongoing team meetings. Each practice was designed to invigorate their prayerful discernment as leaders, which in turn would affect their ability to engage in spiritual discernment together as a team. They seemed to be listening attentively, but it was still too early to tell. We took an overnight retreat together and experienced some of these important disciplines.

The retreat was a bit unusual from what I had previously experienced with other groups, as particularly noted in their lack of involvement in small and large group discussions. I succumbed to the quietness of the group and found myself teaching more than facilitating. The pastor, a key lay leader and I had a handful of discussions off to the side, and they kept urging me on in my approach. But they never explained to me how the members of the group were so intimately related to one another, especially how tied the group was to two very distinct families in the church. Nor did they inform me of the recent history that had brought them to this period of time and how those present for these meetings and on the retreat were vilifying the pastor. In fact—and I do believe they were honest with me at that time—they simply didn't think these facts were relevant.

Until all hell broke loose at the meeting that followed the retreat.

That was when it became crystal clear to me why the group had been so quiet on retreat the previous month. It also became evident that there was a significant problem between members of the team that had been going on for years. The issues brought forth at the meeting, seeping out of the edges of what I thought was a pretty definitive agenda, were voiced loud and clear. Verbal hand grenades were thrown from one side of the table to the other. Historical accusations were leveled to and fro, many of which went back decades. This small church in a rural community had been laced with troubles since its founding just over a century ago.

And, yes, the two currently dominant families had been prevailing all those years. One family, relatively well off, ran a lucrative business in town. The other family came from a farming community just outside the town, now occupying a large family-owned acreage. The feud between them had trickled down two generations. They tolerated one another from a distance but could barely handle being in the same room together. There had been a push-pull tug-of-war between these families as leaders of this small church for decades.

No wonder the chemistry on the retreat seemed a bit odd and stilted to me. Learning about the history of these two families not only made sense of that experience, but it also brought some clarity about the tentative and awkward conversations I had with both the pastor and the key lay leader over the previous two months. They were still sorting out their own reality.

But what I didn't appreciate was the way it all exploded. During this now infamous meeting, when the words were voiced and the emotions began to swell and the pastor and key lay leader were sidelined and the anger began to emerge and the tears were coming and the table was banged and the youngest and most vulnerable stood up and demonstratively left the room and the relatives followed them out the door shouting and screaming—I knew I was in the midst of a feud that had obviously begun much earlier than that night.

I looked over to my left at the pastor, who sat silently, and to the key lay leader, who sat stunned across the table. They both had tears in their eyes and stared back at me. I was in the hot seat. I was dumbfounded. I was saddened and angry myself. I was speechless. I was in charge.

All I knew to do was invite them to pray. I asked a couple people to make sure those who had left in tears were okay to either reenter the room or drive themselves home. The anger-riven atmosphere in the room was quieted by one of the oldest family members present, who suggested firmly that the name calling cease and the anger be silenced—at least for one night. I invited as many who wished to pray to offer their prayers aloud. No one did, so I prayed and asked God for wisdom, strength, compassion and gentleness. I pleaded with the God of love to enter our space and make himself known to each person around the tables. I prayed for a miracle: that division would be healed.

To date my prayers have not been answered. Our ministry didn't work much longer with that church leadership team. Within the next few meetings they rejected our approach. Their divisions widened, and their leaders grew weary. They finally asked the pastor to leave. The church continued to decline in numbers and in its impact in the community.

What I do know, from my relationship with their denominational leader, is that the pastor has found a new place to serve and is thriving today. The church continues to have internal power struggles but is being led by a gracious interim pastor and a denominational reconciliation team who have hope for their future, albeit their very distant future.

As I debriefed this whole experience with my own colleagues, I came to the surprising realization that I too had some repressed anger to deal with. I was angry at the pastor for what felt to me like a set-up. I was angry at the key lay leader for not stepping in and confronting her peers, regardless of how powerful they may have been in their small community. I was angry with myself for not asking more probing questions. I was angry with God for what felt like a failure and a huge waste of my time and energies. My colleagues were terrific, listening well to my heartache and leading me back into a good frame of heart and mind. I now pray regularly for this specific church and many others like them who struggle with relational conflict. Lord, have mercy on your church and the sinful humanity that occupies many a pew today.

When anger is left unmanaged it can ultimately lead to vitriolic hatred. Anger in and among families, in and among the family of God, is untenable without some kind of intervention. And yet it exists in many places today and is often left unchecked for years until it inevitably wreaks havoc on all involved. No wonder the apostle Paul singled out this word as one of the antitheses to love. He was spot on.

LOVE IS NOT EASILY ANGERED

Thankfully, archrival power families aren't everywhere in the life of the church. But they do exist, and they provide an example for us to consider when contemplating our own inclination toward an angry response. Anger is never pretty, even when exhibited as righteous anger, as Jesus expressed when he turned the tables over in the temple that were meant for worship and not for personal economic gain.

Even righteous anger is rarely expressed righteously, since it's difficult to judge the heart rightly and ensure that any anger is undeniably for the good of all. However, it's important to note that an angry response to injustice is the closest we get to Jesus' display of righteous anger. This is especially true if expressed appropriately toward racial discrimination, sex trafficking, irrational hate crimes and abuses of any kind or magnitude. In these instances we need a prayerful, passionate yet professionally guided approach and response. These are not issues to be approached solo or in a haphazard way. Most often, however, in our day-to-day experiences, we need to look anger in the face and identify it for what it truly can become: destructive to relationships and contrary to love.

Where did this word *anger* come from in Paul's exposition of love? Where had he seen it in the churches he had established? Where had he seen it in his own life? The latter question is the easiest to answer, for when he was known as Saul his anger was expressed extravagantly toward any who would disagree with his understanding of righteousness. Especially the new breed of Jesus-followers who had come on the scene and disrupted his life considerably. To them he not only had anger but also hatred, anger's closest sibling.

Paul had obviously seen anger in the divisions of the church in Corinth, calling them out on their quarreling and jealousy and for "acting like mere men" (1 Corinthians 1:10-12; 3:3). Their lack of agreement with one another in general and in the specific issues he addresses dramatically spotlights their anger. The believers in Corinth were living in a culture that was bent on destroying any sign of godliness among them. This is why the newly established church in that city of sin was so greatly challenged to live in a countercultural way. One can only imagine the possibilities of how anger could erupt among the Christians who were seeking to love and serve Jesus in a new and different way in a place like Corinth.

Paul also wrote to the Ephesians about how best to deal with anger. In fact, it's his most pointed teaching on the subject:

> "In your anger do not sin": Do not let the sun go down while you are still angry, and do not give the devil a foothold. . . . Do not let any unwholesome talk come out of your mouths, but only what is helpful for building others up according to their needs, that it may benefit those who listen. And do not grieve the Holy Spirit of God, with whom you were sealed for the day of redemption. Get rid of all bitterness, rage and anger, brawling and slander, along with every form of malice. (Ephesians 4:26-31)

His words to the church in Ephesus parallel what he also said to the believers in Colossae: "But now you must rid yourselves of all such things as these: anger, rage, malice, slander, and filthy language from your lips" (Colossians 3:8). For Paul, it was clear: there is no room in the heart for anger and its accomplices. To each he says, "Do not . . . ," and that mandate is crystal clear to all who heard him speak into their situation and relationships. There was no excuse for prolonged anger that would be perceived as righteous. Instead, he urges his followers to own their anger, even express it as lovingly as possible if need be, but in so doing, to not let the sun go down with anger still residing in the heart.

Paul's teaching is in total alignment with his predecessors in the Old Testament, particularly in the Wisdom literature where God's people are warned that quick-tempered persons display folly and a hot-tempered person produces dissension (Proverbs 14:29; 15:18; 22:24). In fact, there is additional urging not to even associate with one who is easily angered, "do not be quickly provoked in your spirit, for anger resides in the lap of fools" (Ecclesiastes 7:9). Throughout the Scriptures there is no evidence to support an angry person's words or actions, except to acknowledge its presence in personality, attitude, voice and actions. No matter what, unchecked, irrational anger does not belong in the heart of the believer or the faith community. But it certainly exists.

Paul must have realized, however, that anger doesn't just jump out from the heart and issue from the tongue. Anger has deep roots, and it's not easy to relocate such a difficult emotional response. Most angry people were raised in an angry household and thereby carry that tension and begrudging attitude with them wherever they go; they simply don't know any better. Angry people may in fact have been abused verbally, sexually, physically, emotionally or mentally themselves by angry ones who raised or influenced them at home or school or in their neighborhood. To such individuals, the process of expunging anger from their heart may take years of therapy and a lifetime to unlearn. In the most radical situations, we need to be sensitive to expectations as to why these individuals can't just erase anger overnight.

Anger is very complex and difficult to accurately and fully understand. Anger can come from almost any form of rejection, and this is especially true if one has dealt with rejection since childhood or adolescence. Again, such deep-rooted anger is not easily left behind. Anger grows out of patterns of anger expressed by one's perpetrator—and can evoke similar patterns of anger by the recipient, or the opposite: a strong dislike or avoidance of strife of any dimension by the recipient. And strife can emerge from a variety of sources: a harsh judgment, vicious gossip, relentless arguing and ongoing disagreements. Anger can also grow from impatience, especially when people are denied fulfillment of their desires or expectations.

Anger can emerge from a prideful heart and a strong need to be the center of attention. It can come from false accusations or injustices leveled inappropriately against another. Anger comes from unmet needs, usually very basic needs that have been denied since childhood. Additionally, anger comes from favoritism or exclusion and can evoke feelings of being pushed out or left out of the inner circle. And anger can grow out of feelings of envy and/or jealousy when others are getting what they want for themselves. The roots of anger are many, and to expose them can be challenging and hurtful. But in order to begin to deal with anger, its roots must be seriously and prayerfully considered.

Once the roots have been exposed, how do we rid ourselves of anger? For some, Paul's strong word of exhortation, "Do not be angry!" may be enough. But for most, that's just the starting place of awareness and acknowledgment of anger. To build on that, it's important to name the feeling of anger as close to when it occurs as possible and then to identify the experience(s) or perpetrator(s) that evoked it. Why did this situation or person bring out such anger or rage from within your heart? If necessary, seek resolution wherever possible—within your heart, in your relationship with the persons involved, and between you and God—in order to move beyond it both short and long term. "Do not let the sun go down" with anger still hanging on.

Then, prayerfully release the anger you are feeling into the hands of God who desires to carry it for you. As anger erupts in the future, continue to pay close attention to the feeling as it emerges in your heart so that your awareness continues to build. Be sure to ask for help and accountability as needed, as it may be too difficult for you to carry on your own. Also work to avoid any and all forms of shame, blame and self-ridicule if you discover that ridding yourself of anger is one of the largest challenges you've ever faced. You are not alone. People have been struggling with anger since the dawn of time. Anger is resident in our troubled hearts. It rises to the surface and gets expressed more times than we care to admit.

James supports Paul in this regard when he writes, "Be . . . slow to become angry" (James 1:19). What causes such angry fights and quarrels? "Don't they come from your desires that battle within you? You want something but don't get it. You kill and covet, but you cannot have what you want. You quarrel and fight. You do not have, because you do not ask God" (James 4:1-2). The bottom line for all of us in regard to anger or any unhealthy emotional response: ask God. Ask God to show you that he loves you in spite of your anger. Ask God to help you understand the source of your anger. Ask God to lead you to others who can help you: a pastor, counselor, therapist or simply a spiritual friend. Ask God to help you trust him to uproot your anger so that you can obey him without leaning on anger as your first line of defense. There is a more excellent way.

INVITATION TO GENTLE COMPASSION AND EMPATHY

Whether you are dealing with your own anger or the anger of another, it's important to approach this subject with empathy and compassion, and always in a spirit of gentleness. We come with empathy because we are all prone to anger, no matter who we are. Therefore, to look on the anger of another or on your own anger with an empathic heart of understanding and sympathy is key. We must approach anger from the vantage point of "Why?" before looking at the what, who, how, where or when. When we ask why, the most important and most difficult of all questions, we are showing a desire for understanding and transformation. Anything less than this is merely dealing with the surface of anger and not attending to its deep roots. "Why?" helps to identify the root causes of any particular anger or any propensity toward anger. Empathy, the ability to walk in another's shoes, is vital in showing support for the person and situation, especially when it's your own anger.

Compassion is essential because we generally don't purpose to be angry; it's the kind of emotional response that jumps out of our mouths, stirs others up, and exposes more of our heart than anything else. Again, it's rare that anger is truly righteous and acceptable (except toward the injustices we covered earlier). It is mostly hurtful and destructive and therefore needs to be followed up with compassionate forgiveness, grace, kindness and radical transformation. In other words, it must be redeemed.

Therefore, deep trust in God leads us out of an angry disposition into a Christ-centered redemption. Anger, when handled with gentleness of heart, can indeed be replaced by love. If I'm the one who expressed anger, I'm the one responsible to offer a gentle word of apology. If I'm the one who is responsible for bringing out an angry response by my provocation, I'm the one accountable for a gentle attempt at reconciliation. If I'm the one who is the recipient of another's anger, as much as possible I need to look in the eye of my perpetrator with gentleness and forbearance (unless of course this person is out of control; then I must seek appropriate professional counsel, shelter and protection), knowing that person is in the midst of a bad moment and their worst is coming out. I trust that its not to their own liking now or upon reflection. Gentleness of heart is usually the last consideration when anger surfaces, but imagine how different relationships would be if that was our first response rather than all the other defensive alternatives.

My anger in the church story at the beginning of this chapter was more about my fear of failure than about the individuals involved. Anger was the defense of my deeper fear—and this is often the case for all of us. As a leader called to serve a group of angry people, I needed a place to vent my frustration. I didn't have the support or the place to process my anger for a variety of reasons, and upon reflection would have certainly helped me to be more present and effective throughout my time with that team. Left unchecked, anger generally is counterproductive for all concerned.

"Be kind and compassionate to one another, forgiving each other, just as in Christ God forgave you" (Ephesians 4:32). Empathy, compassion, gentleness, forgiveness: combined they make a potion worth consuming so that love can emerge before any form of anger. Let love reign. Let love rule. Let love revive. Let love restore your angry heart.

Spiritual Leadership Audit

Restoring Your Gentle Compassion

Anger is usually a symptom of a deeper heart condition, most likely based in some form of fear. We become angry when someone or something provokes our verbal or visceral responses in ways that can be destructive to ourselves and others who witness our anger. When angry people take time to consider the reasons they become angry, they can indeed be transformed from the inside out. However, when they refuse to look in the mirror of the heart and decline opportunities for reflection, brokenness, repentance and renewal, they will continue to exhibit unhealthy anger. What is your choice, dear leader and servant of Jesus? A gentle leader is far more productive in the kingdom of God than one who allows anger to permeate, penetrate and punctuate their heart and spill out angry vomit on their relationships. As you approach the following exercises, pray that God will soften your heart as you deal honestly with this all-important emotional and relational topic.

Confess your brokenness: Naming your brokenness and owning it as a present reality.

- In what way(s) have you found yourself angry, or experienced anger from another, most recently?

- Consider prayerfully the details of this experience and recount them here.

Rest and trust in God's abiding presence and peace: Seeking God's gentleness to be revealed and released from within your soul.

- *Hopeful in Scripture*: Read through Paul's longest treatment of the subject of anger, Ephesians 4:25-32. Recount the times you allowed the sun to go down before your anger was resolved.

- *Faithful in prayer*: Ask God for his wisdom and strength to carry you forward in resolving not to let the sun go down with anger lingering in your heart. What is standing in the way for you today?

- *Thankful in reflection*: Take note of your key relationships. Who in your life receives the least of your anger? Why? Who in your life receives most of your anger? Why? Any invitation to change that in the future?

Invite God to redeem your brokenness: Restoring God's gentle compassion in you. As Christian leaders, it's helpful to note that our prayer book, the Psalms, is filled with language that sounds a lot like anger! Rest assured that in your own prayers, expressing anger is something God can handle. Find freedom in your prayer to vent and express any and all of your anger, and then ask God to be the one to enlighten and heal your angry heart, especially as you are called to deal relationally with others in your sphere of influence. Giving yourself this permission will open up new doors of service to others as you grant them similar permission to express themselves fully, honestly and emotionally with God.

In order for you to attend to your anger as a leader and intend instead to embody God's gentleness and compassion toward others, you may need to sit with the word *forgiveness* before proceeding to the next subject. Either jot notes here or in a journal, as most anger needs to be forgiven.

- Any forgiveness needing to be expressed between you and God?

- Any forgiveness needing to be expressed between you and others?

- Any forgiveness needing to be expressed toward yourself?

- What does gentleness look like for you? What will it take to get to the place where gentle compassion fully replaces your anger? Who will you invite to graciously, prayerfully and lovingly hold you accountable in this desire?

(Note that the topic of anger can reveal deep-seated issues that require professional care from a trusted therapist or trained conflict resolver.)

- eight -

The Truth Always Sets Us Free

Love keeps no record of wrongs, does not delight in evil,
but rejoices in truth

ZACH'S LEADERSHIP POSITION in his nonprofit setting was what many would call a dream come true. He was invited to serve in this capacity after an extensive interview process and a unanimous vote of the board of directors. His credentials were spotless, with all the right degrees from some of the best academic institutions and skills that would perfectly match the setting and the role. The early months of his tenure were smooth and effective. Everyone seemed pleased.

However, at the six-month mark the situation began to turn sour. The relationships on the board, which previously had been united and energetic, were beginning to wane. The staff team, which Zach inherited, began to wonder if their future was as bright as was promised when their new leader came on board.

It was during the staff and one-on-one meetings with Zach that questions began to emerge. In the early weeks it seemed rather harmless, but as time kept rolling along, the number of questions kept increasing. He liked to use humor to make his points, but far too often his opinion about what was funny wasn't shared by all. Zach's stories were about others, mostly those with whom he had served in his previous work setting.

When the various senior members of Zach's new team had their scheduled alone time with Zach, they began to hear stories about their peers. Zach thought it humorous to put blame on others by putting them down and speaking ill of their performance. In open office settings he would even use his form of (perceived) humor to shame others publicly.

Over time, the uncomfortable feeling in meetings with Zach increased. Chatter among the staff had one major theme: Zach's insecurity as a leader was most pronounced in his ability to deflect responsibility from him to others by what had become a rather masterful use of blaming and shaming. Ironically, he thought it was funny and would laugh hysterically with himself while telling his tales. But it began to undermine unity and destroy productivity.

His background and family of origin influenced his ill-placed sense of humor and his propensity to shame others. That was what he experienced growing up in his rather dysfunctional family, and he used such tactics in athletics, academics and among many of his acquaintances. So with no previous senior leadership experience and a tainted family background, Zach was a bit oblivious to how he was coming across to his new team.

Zach's leadership began to fall off the tracks when he would blame and shame his followers for not doing as he asked and thereby leave his expectations unfulfilled. Each time there was a consultation with Zach regarding his leadership challenges, he would offer a litany of other people's wrongs. He had them memorized. And he was a master at using his words to ridicule others while consistently defending himself.

He used his powerful role to manipulate people and situations to his own end. He used his forceful voice to intimidate. And he used his strong personality to cover up his own mistakes and instead blame others. He spoke against others on the team in derogatory and inflammatory ways and rather indiscriminately and inappropriately.

Finally the board confronted him. They hired a firm that specializes in conflict resolution to step in and meet with Zach one-on-one. The conflict resolvers interviewed the senior team and invited their feedback. Zach was firmly encouraged to receive their loving rebuke through the specificity of details shared. At first he was defensive, but during the process his heart began to soften toward those who spoke truth in a gracious manner. There was no condemnation, only a desire to find equilibrium to once again focus on their vision and mission and not on the failures of others.

Remarkably and thankfully in this case, Zach had an awakening that led to a major turnaround for his leadership. He listened intently to all the comments about his leadership, both the positives as well as the areas of greatest concern. He confessed his mean-spiritedness and sought professional counsel to address both past and present relationships. He repented of his poor use of humor, confessed his blaming and shaming, and sought forgiveness from his board and team. It was a wake-up call of epic proportion for Zach and the entire organization, and it was a turnaround that ignited the team.

Today Zach is still working on his personal growth plan and is thriving in this environment. He is a changed man, transformed from the inside out. There is no longer any manipulative arrogance in his heart or in the hearts of others on his team. It's a beautiful picture of redemption and reconciliation, based in how this leader was willing to own his actions, submit his heart to God and the people he was called to serve, and seek a new way of living and leading among them. His transformation has become all-important not only to him but also to many of his peers in other leadership settings. He's written and spoken on this topic in conference settings. The fruit of his deep inner soul work has produced a work environment filled with grace and peace.

LOVE KEEPS NO RECORD OF WRONGS, DOES NOT DELIGHT IN EVIL, BUT REJOICES IN THE TRUTH

As much as the truth may hurt, it's always best to unearth, represent, own and speak the truth in love. The truth will always set you free, whether it's the truth of the gospel message itself or the truth about a situation, decision, organization, person—or about yourself as a leader. Lies and exaggerations are never good alternatives. Despite this world of "spin," it's dangerous for leaders to embrace a posture of twisting, realigning or even slightly misrepresenting the truth. But boards, leaders and teams are naturally and humanly inclined toward such behavior in order to protect whatever falsehood or lack of success is being managed behind the scenes.

Zach's change of heart is primarily a reflection of the positive ripple effects of an environment that exhibits grace. In that merciful place Zach could be coached and edified as the truth was spoken lovingly and confrontationally to him about his unhealthy attitude. Since Zach is a leader after God's heart, his openness to receive rebuke and correction is what saved him in the long run. Left to his own unhealthy attitudes and inappropriate verbal expressions, Zach would have self-destructed as a leader. But thanks be to God, not only was his role spared, but also the entire organization was protected in reputation and fruitfulness.

We see truth spoken in love by the apostle Paul when he raises his concerns to the church in Corinth. He spends the majority of 1 and 2 Corinthians speaking into and correcting the people of God in several aspects of their shared life and ministry. In addressing the issues, he speaks with clarity and conviction but never with an attitude of condemnation by way of shaming or blaming (1 Corinthians 4:14). He calls the Corinthians to account for their attitudes, values and actions, and provides a path out of the quagmires he identifies.

He continually reminds them to speak the truth about the gospel they profess and to live truthfully in every aspect of their individual and shared lives as believers in Jesus. In seeking to ward off divisions in the body, Paul reminds them that each are God's temple, and that the Spirit of God lives in them (1 Corinthians 3:16). God's temple is sacred, therefore their lives are to be holy: "Do not deceive yourselves. If any one of you thinks he is wise by the standards of this age, he should become a 'fool' so that he may become wise. For the wisdom of this world is foolishness in God's sight. As it is written: 'He catches the wise in their craftiness'" (1 Corinthians 3:18-19).

Paul's strong warning against being lured by the world's craftiness is further delineated in the expulsion of the immoral brother in chapter 5: "A man has his father's wife. And you are proud! Shouldn't you rather have been filled with grief and have put out of your fellowship the many who did this?" (1 Corinthians 5:1-2). The obvious inclusion of inappropriate sexual practices among the Corinthians has led them into living a lie: they had somehow reconciled these sexual deviations as acceptable in their hearts and minds. And the preponderance of such activity was not only affecting their individual lifestyles but polluting the entire body of Christ. "Therefore let us keep the Festival [for Christ, our Passover lamb], not with the old yeast, the yeast of malice and wickedness, but with bread without yeast, the bread of sincerity and truth" (1 Corinthians 5:8).

Paul addresses the Corinthians' sexual immorality head-on. There is no mincing of words from the apostle in this regard. They were living a lie, delighting in evil rather than rejoicing in the truth. Their sexual practices embody most clearly the evil rampant among them. Paul speaks to that issue in several poignant ways, but his message is always crisp and clear:

> The body is not meant for sexual immorality. . . . Flee from sexual immorality. All other sins a man commits are outside the body, but he who sins sexually sins against his own body. Do you not know that your body is a temple of the Holy Spirit, who is in you, whom you have received from God? You are not your own; you were bought with a price. Therefore honor God with your body. (1 Corinthians 6:13, 18-20)

It's fascinating to see how Paul boldly addresses the subject of sexual immorality. It's the curse of our age as well, prevalent in so many sectors of our society, including the church, and it needs to be addressed for the evil it embodies. So often it's the place where leaders hide, remaining in bondage to the flesh. Giving voice to such deceit is the beginning of freedom from the inside out.

All lies aren't sexual in nature, to be sure, but the most sensitive area of truthfulness (or lack thereof) affects all other aspects of relationships, decision making and integrity for living the God-centered life. May the church be purified from such evil, and may we be bold enough to be united around addressing this and any other subject that hinders a life of truth-telling. For the glory of God and the building up of his kingdom here on earth, let us all choose to live with truthful integrity.

Paul's goal for all the churches he planted and grew toward maturity was for them to always live to honor God in every way. It was the same for the church in Corinth, "so we make it our goal to please him" (2 Corinthians 5:9). This means that everyone was to be treated as one who has taken on the life that Christ invites. No longer swept into the world's ways of being, the church of Jesus Christ is to live fully, rigorously and completely for God alone.

INVITATION TO RECONCILIATION

According to the apostle Paul, the ministry that leaders and followers alike are to absorb is that of reconciliation. The grace, mercy and forgiveness of Christ are treasured gifts that reconcile us to God, and it's those same gifts that reconcile us to one another, and even to ourselves:

> For Christ's love compels us, because we are convinced that one died for all, and therefore all died. . . . Therefore, if anyone is in Christ, he is a new creation; the old has gone, the new has come! All this is from God, who reconciled us to himself through Christ and gave us the ministry of reconciliation: that God was reconciling the world to himself in Christ, not counting men's sins against them. And he has committed to us the message of reconciliation. We are therefore Christ's ambassadors, as though God were making his appeal through us. (2 Corinthians 5:14-20)

Reconciliation is the message of transformed lives focused on building the kingdom of God truthfully, from the inside out.

When we befriend our brokenness—that which keeps us from full fellowship with God—we come to grips with our own propensity toward shaming and blaming, pointing fingers and accusing others of issues we need to own for ourselves. To be

reconciled is to be a grateful recipient of the grace, mercy and
tender forgiveness of God made available to us in Christ alone.
As we posture ourselves to receive this tremendous gift from the
loving hand of God, our lives are changed from the inside out.
Truth always sets us free.

Reconciliation is the best one-word definition for all of ministry leadership. I repeat this over and over again with the young
leaders I mentor. The term *reconciliation* sums up the message
of the gospel, the mission of the church, and the ministry of
leaders and teams. It's a key expression to understand for all
believers who are serious about fulfilling God's abundant will
for our lives. To be reconciled means that no matter what we
have said or done, no matter the geography we have traversed to
date, we are given a second chance. And it's offered to us because
we are loved by and invited to know and serve the God of second
chances. *Reconciliation* is an excellent summation of grace,
mercy and forgiveness. It's a defining word for how we are to live
as kingdom builders in our own generation—always.

When I am reconciled with *God*, I am a grateful recipient of
his generous gifts of grace, mercy and forgiveness. This occurs
when I finally realize I am not a god or guardian of my life but
instead am dependent on the power of God alone to redeem the
pain of my brokenness.

When I am reconciled with *others*, I am a generous distributor
of his grace, mercy and forgiveness, whether or not it's received
by another. For those of us who call ourselves Christian, we have
an obligation to be reconcilers in all of our relationships.

When I am reconciled with *myself*, I am a godly prompter of
his grace, mercy and forgiveness first and foremost for myself.
In the care of my own heart and soul, I need the deep-down daily
reminders that no matter what my sinful lot in life may become,
I am always a dearly loved child of God. To know in my heart of

hearts that I am beloved of the Father in heaven, reconciled forever because of the redemptive work of Christ and renewed daily in the presence and power of the Spirit, is the most life-giving reminder of all.

INVITATION TO TRUTH-TELLING

Some may consider spinning a story more like a *half-truth* than a full-out *lie*. But half-truths can lead one down the alley of deception rather swiftly. When leaders in particular begin to receive and communicate half-truths, they are walking the fine line between good and evil. How they handle such inconsistencies around specific story lines will influence their effectiveness in the service of others. When leaders are caught in such a conundrum of "spin," they walk more of a tightrope of faithfulness to God and others. The potential of a serious fall into the abyss of outright falsehood is heightened. When we excuse such behavior as innocent, we are collaborating with the guilty party, which is dangerous as well.

There are times when we get confused through the hearing of *false doctrines* or *false promises* from spiritual leaders. For the unlearned and innocent ears, this may be difficult to distinguish. But for those who sit under such teaching and are literate of the truths in God's Word, there is a corresponding responsibility to address such falsehoods and bring them to a halt. When a false understanding of God is presented or proposed, our minds and hearts must be protected by the true God.

Hypocrisy is another form of evil that grows out of living falsely among others. This is when we say one thing but live another. The hypocrite among us, and often within us, must be watched carefully so that this disease doesn't spread like wildfire. When we pretend to be something we're not, we give others the impression that we're holier than we actually are. We look haughtily down on others and, in turn, live behind a false front, presenting ourselves to others in a way that distorts our image and deceives them.

Hypocrites often struggle to defend themselves and so live with a form of *self-deception*. To be self-deceived is to believe "truths" about ourselves that are actually false. On the other end of the deception continuum is *flattery*, which is speaking falsely of another in charming and manipulative ways. When we are flattering, we are seeking to win others over by saying whatever it takes to bolster them up.

Outright lies are the worst of the bunch. These are spoken with deliberate intent. To lie to another is to belittle the relationship to the lowest denominator. All that's left is presence, which is blackened and marred and often without repute. When people lie, they are purposefully walking away from any legitimate form of personal integrity and entering into the land of deception. A lying tongue is something that God hates, and so should we. To tolerate the toxic concoction of direct, face-to-face lies is to choose to reside with the enemy of our souls, the author of evil himself. It's an abomination to our personhood and should be avoided at all costs.

It's difficult to recover after being found out as a liar and a fraud. But it's not impossible. The way out is to eradicate all tendencies to spin or lie about our life or the institutions and organizations we represent. It takes a deliberate choice of the will to cease spreading falsehoods by way of half-truths, spins or outright lies. It takes a holy conviction and humble courage to admit such a wrong way of living among others in the body of Christ. But the only reversal away from a life of evil deception is toward confession of such a sin, accompanied by an earnest desire to live, speak and relate truthfully and uprightly at all times. It takes a fresh move of God's Spirit to unleash such an attitude and the righting of the devastating course of lying.

Since love does not delight in evil, it indeed flourishes in truth. Rejoicing in truths about God and ourselves can bring about an abundance of life on earth. It's a serious blunder to live in the world of "spin" or half-truths, as they only grow into evil intentions and, ultimately, lies. But it's a hopeful blessing to be released from the spirit of lies and ushered into the arms of the Spirit of truth. Welcome home, truth-speaker, to the heart of the Almighty One, the author of truth and the giver of life.

Spiritual Leadership Audit

Restoring Your Grace, Mercy and Forgiveness

Keeping a record of wrongs is a miserable way to live. When we stoop to the low place of counting up how many times others have wronged us, we only wreak mayhem on the soul. Adding up sins committed against us will keep us from seeing how we contribute to those sins, and we will miss the gifts of confession, forgiveness, grace, mercy and love. As you consider your own possible propensity to shaming and blaming others, be gentle with yourself and invite God's healing balm of grace, mercy and forgiveness to flood your soul.

The truth will set you free—always. Not only does the truth of the gospel of Jesus set us free; so does the truth about ourselves, those who surround us and the situations we all share in life. To avoid truth is to embrace a false reality, which can lead us into the downward spiral of deception. Let me encourage you to ask the Lord to forgive you for rejoicing or delighting in any evil when the call on our lives as Christians is to shun and deliberately shut out evil from its infectious and destructive powers. Sit prayerfully and openhandedly with the following reflections and invite the Spirit of Christ to rest over your soul and grant you the gifts of grace-filled reconciliation and authentic truth-telling you long for. Then deliver the same to others in your many orbits of influence.

Confess your brokenness: Naming your brokenness and owning it as a present reality.

- In what way(s) have you found yourself shaming and blaming others, or experiencing shame and blame from another, most recently?

- In what way(s) have you found yourself delighting in a false-hood about God, another person or even yourself, or experiencing falsehood from another, most recently?

- Consider prayerfully the details of this experience and recount them here.

Rest and trust in God's abiding presence and peace: Seeking God's reconciliation and truth to be revealed and released from within your soul.

- *Hopeful in Scripture*: Ponder the meaning of reconciliation as the apostle Paul outlines its importance in 2 Corinthians 5:14-20. Pay attention to how the Word draws you nearer to the heart of God in the area of reconciliation. How is truth-telling important to all meaningful reconciliation?

- *Faithful in prayer*: In what way(s) is your heart strangely warmed to the ministry of reconciliation? Ask the Spirit of truth to reveal whatever resides in your heart that is harboring any form of falsehood in your attitude, character or relationship with others.

- *Thankful in reflection*: Consider one person in your life who needs to be reconciled to God or someone (possibly you) in the body of Christ. How are you being urged to be a vessel of reconciliation? Is there any action you are invited to fulfill with grace and humility of heart?

Invite God to redeem your brokenness: Restoring God's loving work of reconciliation and truth in you.

- Grace is never earned, and rarely is it deserved. From whom are you withholding such a gift, and what are you waiting for?

- Mercy is best delivered tenderly and compassionately. What is blocking your soul from receiving affectionate mercy from God during this season of life?

- Forgiveness is a gift we offer and receive. Where in your heart is there a deep need for God's loving forgiveness? Toward whom is there an invitation to offer or request forgiveness?

- It's important to acknowledge three important truths about oneself: I am dearly loved by God the Creator, Redeemer, Sustainer and Transformer of my life; I am deeply sinful and in need of daily, prayerful recognition of this reality; and when I am in submission to the Lover of my soul, who will rescue me out of darkness and travel with me down the road of renewal and transformation, I know that this process of sanctification will take a lifetime to fulfill. In what way can you embrace these all-important and life-transforming truths and abide in them today? In the coming week? Over a lifetime?

- nine -

When Fear and Worry Ensnare a Heart

Love always protects

FOR NEARLY FORTY YEARS NOW, I've been in ministry leadership capacities in local church, parachurch, nonprofit and academic settings. I've had the privilege of serving with four incredible organizations over those years. But our family hasn't needed to move geographically even though I've left one place and shifted emphasis to another. Saying goodbye and leaving but never moving out of town isn't as easy as it sounds. In fact it can be rather heart wrenching, especially relationally, as we needed to shift emphasis from one group of people to the next.

When our family moved on from our eleven years of pastoral ministry on the team at Grace Chapel (Lexington, Massachusetts) and I stepped into the role of president of the Evangelistic Association of New England (EANE, which became known as Vision New England during my fourteen-year tenure), it was a big move and a major shift in responsibilities for me in more ways than one. In addition, our family was still being formed:

our son, Nathan, was only four years old, and our daughter, Rebekah, was soon to be born.

When I was approached to assume this new role, Ruth and I actually prayed that God would close the door. It seemed like too large of a leap, too demanding of a role, and we felt too young to lead this one-hundred-year-old organization. But the more we prayed, God made his will crystal clear and kept opening wide the door for us to move in that direction. The decision was affirmed by the board of directors at EANE and among our group of trusted confidantes at the church.

The night we were blessed and sent by the congregation was filled with joy, thanksgiving and many wonderful memories. The church did an awesome job of lavishing love, affection and affirmation on our family as they offered their thanks and prayed blessing over our family for our hope-filled success. It was a glorious moment. But it was also one filled with anxiety, worry and fear.

At the reception held in our honor, after the last few congregants came through the receiving line, I noticed out of the corner of my eye my beautiful, pregnant wife following our son, Nate, around the fellowship hall. Nate had a new limp to his gate as he walked and tried to run around the room with his friends. We were leaving the next morning for a much-needed vacation break in between jobs, and my heart sank with profound heaviness. Here we were being celebrated by a generous, loving church family, and all I could think about was my son's health.

Shortly after Nate's first birthday, we discovered a congenital defect in his right leg. He had surgery immediately thereafter. Our Grace Chapel family circled around us for this surgery and a handful more hospitalizations and surgeries in subsequent years. They had prayed for us and for his healing countless times. Just prior to our departure, we thought he was in an upswing regarding the health of his right leg. But on this night, what Ruth and I feared the most—another bone broken and another surgery—seemed inevitable. We left the next day on our vacation, and as the time progressed his limp got worse. We called the doctors from our hotel room to ensure an appointment immediately upon our arrival home. Within a few short weeks he was back in surgery once again.

Leaving a job and church we loved, moving into a new and daunting leadership role on top of facing surgery for our son and preparing for the arrival of a new child in a few short months were a few of the stressors that fell on us overnight. In addition, gray skies and springtime rains were drenching our area, causing latent sadness in our hearts. The EANE offices were in Boston, so I was commuting on the subway each day, and battling impatient crowds wasn't helpful for my soul. During the days Nate was at Children's Hospital I would commute from the hospital to my office and then spend the nights with him in his room while Ruth got much needed rest as a pregnant mother at home. They were dark and lonely days for us, adding anxiety and fear to our newly overwhelmed lives.

When September rolled around, our dear daughter was born. Rebekah's arrival was symbolic of a change in seasons for all of us. Her beautiful face radiated joy, and our lives began to return to a new normal. Nate was back on his feet (although his physical challenges would continue to recur for several more years, until, as a senior in high school, the surgeries came to an end and we were able to watch him graduate and move on splendidly in his life). Ruth was flourishing as a young mom once more. And I was beginning to understand more fully the role I was to play in leadership at EANE.

The transition to an expanded leadership role was both exhausting and exhilarating. The challenges were immense:

serving as editor of a monthly newspaper, raising much-needed funds, planning large conferences, leading a diverse staff team, finding new office space and developing relationships with a whole new constituency, all of which were perplexing for me. There were times I was overwrought with worry, saddled with anxiety, overwhelmed with fear. Would I fail and become the laughing stock of the Christian community? Would I feel pressured to make any number of untenable decisions? Would I make it in this nonprofit parachurch world that was so unfamiliar to me and so different from local church life?

Were it not for the people God sent my way to companion me during this traumatic season, I'm not sure how the story would have ended. I thank God for the EANE board and friends like David who left his corporate job and took over our finances. He accompanied me on many a commute, willingly made sense out of the piles of disorganized papers in the office, listened to me rant about my challenges and perceived shortcomings, and helped me sort out various options in order to make informed and intelligent decisions. I'm forever grateful.

To be known as an anxious, worried, fear-filled leader leaves those you are leading in a vulnerable spot. When any form of anxiety is present, regardless of its root in the heart of a leader, an atmosphere of protection and trust is generally absent. Those who follow such a leader often acquire some of his or her insecurities, while others push back and fight off absorbing such an attitude. To admit to oneself and others that you struggle with such anxiety is brave and courageous. When you have companionship with colleagues who care and assurance of the call from God, the one who matters most, it's incredible to watch how such fears can be washed away. To be loved into leadership and protected by the Spirit and a healthy Christian community is the best way forward no matter the obstacles standing in the way.

LOVE ALWAYS PROTECTS

It's fascinating to note that when Paul came to the Corinthian church, he came "in weakness and fear" (1 Corinthians 2:3). He didn't come "with eloquence or superior wisdom" as he proclaimed to them the testimony about God. "For [he] resolved to know nothing while [he] was with [them] except Jesus Christ and him crucified" (1 Corinthians 2:2). His message and preaching were not "with wise and persuasive words, but with a demonstration of the Spirit's power, so that [their] faith might not rest on men's wisdom, but on God's power" (1 Corinthians 2:4-5). These are comforting words to contemplate as an imperfect leader.

Paul had a protective attitude toward the Corinthians. He was there to protect the gospel of Jesus Christ, to protect and preserve the work that had been growing in that city, and to become a powerful witness for Christ. In all of his teaching and serving in their midst, he was there to protect the purity of the message of Christ and the sanctified lifestyle of those who were called to follow Christ. He was there to protect them as brothers and sisters in Christ.

But there were so many issues to address with the church in that secular city that Paul needed to speak with honesty and veracity. His holy boldness was matched with Spirit-empowered courage, for protecting the gospel required a bullish commitment to Christ in a place of such sinful disposition and opposition. Paul would not have accomplished what he set out to do if he was a bully, pushing his weight around and arrogantly stampeding over the leaders and people who were recognized as Christ-followers. Instead, his courageous confidence in Christ matched the strength of his vital and timely message to the leaders and church in Corinth.

In essence, Paul was called to Corinth to protect them from the worst parts of themselves. That's what protective leadership looked like then, and now. It's not so much about the strength of the leader but about the wisdom being expounded by the leader, embraced by the team and then entrusted to the followers. Leaders like Paul are essential if the church is to be preserved and expanded with the gospel of Jesus as its centerpiece. Paul admitted to the Corinthians that he came with weakness and fear, and with much trembling. He knew that he had an enormous task to accomplish among them, and therefore he needed to entrust his leadership into the hands of the all-wise God who called and equipped him by the Spirit for this incredible undertaking.

Paul's protective stance was forged out of the two-sided coin of human weakness and Spirit empowerment. If he came to bully them forcefully into obedience, he would not have gotten very far. A bullying edge in leadership does nothing but promote the insecurities of the leader and evoke unhealthy fear among the followers. Paul's goal was clearly focused on the preservation of the gospel in Corinth and the sanctifying work of the Spirit among those who had already claimed the name of Christ.

Paul was a protector and preserver of the early church everywhere God sent him. In each of his missionary journeys Paul expressed urgency for living distinctly Christian lives among the culturally secular landscapes where those churches were being formed. And each church—whether in Corinth, Philippi, Ephesus, Thessalonica or Rome—was distinct in its issues, and Paul knew what to address every step of the way. He invested his leadership life in understanding specific needs and concerns, issues and conflicts, personalities and propensities, and he spoke boldly and lovingly to each church under his care.

In many respects it was Barnabas who launched Paul into the public eye as the first-century church's central leadership role. His colleague Barnabas was the first to speak up for Paul's genuine conversion, and that advanced his fatherly role in the early church. Paul was protected by Barnabas and others who saw the evidence of his newfound faith in Jesus, his ability to communicate the gospel with powerful intensity and his tireless commitment to see the mission of Jesus advanced throughout the world. Paul's mission was to lovingly protect and preserve the gospel of Jesus Christ.

The Corinthians who would hear his message and be provoked by his promptings to return to a life of faithfulness would come to realize his lovingly protective ways. He was firm and resilient, all the while clear and charismatic. And he was always present to encourage their well-being, their unity and their fruitfulness for the kingdom of God.

INVITATION TO REPLACE FEAR, ANXIETY AND WORRY WITH PEACE

The Lord Jesus provided protective love and care for his disciples. His invitation to come close, draw near and follow him was both individual and communal. He was sent to protect his followers from the worst part of themselves as well. His mission, message and ministry were always for the betterment of his disciples. He consistently spoke peace into their fearful hearts, which would lead others into a life-changing faith that was bathed in his peace.

One of the more dramatic moments the disciples had with Jesus came in the middle of a storm at sea. In Matthew 8, Luke 8 and Mark 4, we find Jesus and his disciples leaving the crowds behind and heading over to the other side of the lake. During their seafaring journey, they encounter two storms: one that

came in the form of a furious squall and the other that came
from within the disquieted hearts of his disciples.

During both the weather and the worry storms, Jesus is asleep
in the back of the boat. When the disciples wake him up, exas-
perated by his restfulness, they cry out with a collective sigh,
"Teacher, don't you care if we drown?" (Mark 4:38). When he got
up from his abbreviated nap, he calms the winds with the words,
"Quiet! Be still!" (Mark 4:39). He settles down his fear-filled disciples with the comforting and protective words, "Why are you
so afraid? Do you still have no faith?" (Mark 4:40). They are
dumbfounded by his terrifying ability to quiet the storm's vio-
lent winds and, more significantly, his incredible insight into
their storm-ravaged and troubled souls.

Paul's ministry in Corinth was marked by the same mysterious work of the Spirit of Christ. His message of wisdom and
strength came not from the insights of human rulers of his age
but instead from "God's secret wisdom, a wisdom that has been
hidden and that God destined for our glory before time began.
None of the rulers of this age understood it, for if they had, they
would not have crucified the Lord of glory. . . . For . . . no one
knows the thoughts of God except the Spirit of God. . . . But we
have the mind of Christ" (1 Corinthians 2:7-8, 11, 16). Paul's protective leadership in Corinth was to remind the church to lean
fully into the trustworthy yet mysterious work of Christ. The
strength and wisdom of Christ outweighed their inadequate
human strength and wisdom, and the work of Christ's Spirit
would transform and protect their very lives.

Jesus and Paul offer an alternative to the fears and worries of
this life: a peace that surpasses all understanding. A peace that
would guide and guard their hearts and minds. A peace that no
storm would ever be able to destroy. A peace that comes solely
by trusting the Lord of peace, who came to bring peace out of

every stormy gale. A peace that the world will never know, but one that can be seen, known and lived fully by the ones who choose to follow Jesus. A peace that emerges in the heart of a leader embracing his anxiety and relying on Jesus.

The invitation Jesus is offering his anxious disciples in the midst of their storm and the invitation Paul issued to the early church is the same invitation we are to offer one another: trust Jesus to press peace into this often-troubled life. For all of life is learning about trust: trusting God and learning how best to trust others and even ourselves, so that when trust is breached, we can embrace our propensity toward worry, anxiety and fear and find our restoration in the peaceful presence of Christ. The peace of Christ guards our hearts and protects our relationships.

Often our fears arise when we feel lonely or abandoned, unprotected by God or insecure among significant others in our lives. Anxiety can also come from a variety of sources. We worry about our image; we get concerned about paying the bills; we fear the future or anything that's unknown. We have times when worry is well founded, as in times of war or catastrophe or epic storms or economic crisis. But we also have times in our life when the worry is unmerited by our inadvertent internal angst or overwhelmed by out-of-control external life circumstances. Our fears may seem irrational in hindsight, but at the time they occur they are very real. To whisk away our fears, anxieties or worries can at times feel mostly impossible, but we must learn to embrace them as our lived reality. Only then will they be set free and redeemed for God's glory.

For the first disciples, the gale-force winds of the storm rocked their little boat. For each of them, there was also a storm raging within their anxious and wondering hearts. But in the midst of the storms, we find the disciples encouraged by Jesus to embrace the quiet stillness accompanied by the faith and peace that Christ alone can provide. In the calming of the storms Jesus reminds them they are dearly loved. He restores their confidence in him by protecting them from the worst of themselves.

Leaders who choose to protect their followers will always put themselves in harm's way first in order to shield others from the storms of life. They will also stand beside those who are ravaged by life's tumult and offer words of hope and actions that evoke peace. And they will encourage by example what it means to cast our worries, fears and anxieties at the feet of Jesus, knowing with great and growing certainty that our peace can only be found in him.

However, leaders must first identify the places within themselves that are filled with worry, fear and anxiety. As leaders, do we feel protected by the peace that surpasses all understanding? Are we filled to overflowing with a trusting peace that sustains us in all the storms of life, or are we being bullied to fight the storms with all our human might? To openhandedly place our worst and deepest fears into the peace-filled hands of Jesus is the only way to experience tender submission and restored faith.

Spiritual Leadership Audit

Restoring Your Inner Reservoir of Peace

Perhaps this chapter has brought to the surface some of your most deeply held fears, worries or anxieties. Confessing them before the Lord is where you will find refreshment and peace for your troubled soul. If you are willing to befriend your fears and get up close and personal with each of them, Jesus will breathe new life into your ongoing pursuit of inner peace. He will restore his peace in the deepest recesses of your heart and soul. Will you allow him full access to do so as he desires? Receive the embrace of your Savior today and watch how his peace saturates your life and relationships, your service and witness, your generosity and grace. Although you may be thinking Jesus is asleep in the back of your boat and oblivious to your concerns, think again. With childlike wonder, joy, peace and faith, consider all the many ways he's actually quite alert. Let Jesus grant you his peace.

Confess your brokenness: Naming your brokenness and owning it as a present reality.

- In what way(s) have you found yourself bullying, or bullied by others, or filled with worry, fear or anxiety most recently?

- Consider prayerfully the details of this experience and recount them here.

Rest and trust in God's abiding presence and peace: Seeking God's peace to be revealed and released from within your soul.

- *Hopeful in Scripture*: Reread Mark 4:35-41, when Jesus calms the storms.

- *Faithful in prayer*: How can you relate to the disciples' question, "Teacher, don't you care if we drown?" and personalize it to your current situation(s) of fear?

- *Thankful in reflection*: Reflect on the places where fear, worry or anxiety come to the surface most frequently for you. Ponder who or what evokes these to occur. How would a deeper faith in Jesus reorder these heart concerns?

Invite God to redeem your brokenness: Restoring God's loving peace in you. We are called to protect ourselves and those within our care from the ongoing wiles of the enemy. In times of stress, we are not to succumb to the temptation to bully or overpower others. Instead, we are called to press peace into unsettled circumstances, troubled relationships and concerned souls. To practice such protection requires ongoing spiritual discernment. Like the apostle Paul, we too need to trust the empowering presence of the Holy Spirit to guide, sustain and protect. The work of the Spirit in troubled times is at minimum the offering of wisdom, protection and peace. Consider how best to activate these God provisions during this season of life and service.

- *Wisdom*: In what ways are you seeking God's wisdom and strength today?

- *Protection*: In what ways are you sensing God's protection over your life, ministry, business or relationships?

- *Peace*: In what ways are you submitting to God's oversight of your life so that you can trust in his peace during any storm that may come your way?

- ten -

The Pitfalls of Needing to Be Wanted

Love always trusts

EVERYONE WALKING PLANET EARTH SHARES a common need—to be fully known, loved, appreciated, affirmed, celebrated and, very simply, wanted. In families first and foremost and then in friendships, neighborhoods, schools, churches, businesses and every other social setting we find ourselves in, the same need remains. Further, it tends to both deepen and grow as the years progress, especially if not provided early in life. There's something so fundamental to this core need that it often goes unstated or underestimated and, unfortunately, can either be naturally and genuinely dispensed, or illogically and grossly ignored.

That's where the story of Charlotte comes in. Charlotte grew up in a household where insecurity grew like a germ in a petri dish. Her parents were well known in the community where she was raised, but behind the scenes it wasn't pretty. Her father was always emotionally absent, leaving the raising of Charlotte and her two younger siblings to her mother. But her mother was emotionally unstable, unfit for parenting since she had been torpedoed by her own set of challenges. She had been raised by an abusive father, always angry at life since the day his wife, Charlotte's grandmother, died when Charlotte's mother was just a baby herself. Not a good recipe for successful family health and relational dynamics.

Everything Charlotte remembers about her childhood is painful. She was the oldest of the three children and the "whipping girl" of the family. If there was a person to blame or to take out aggression on, it was always Charlotte. She bore the brunt of her mother's frustrations for as long as she can recall. She rarely had a happy day at home; never does she recall a fun holiday, and she has no recollection of birthday parties or owning a teddy bear. The exceptions to the unpleasant moments were always outside the home, among friends, at school, church and in the community.

Most of her life was filled with stress, anxiety and insecurity. Home was a place of conditional acceptance and uncontrolled anger. Charlotte rarely knew safety and security in her home and never could anticipate when the next shoe would drop or the next explosion would erupt. This led to her continually feeling excluded, abandoned and rejected from the very persons who should be providing the opposite for her. This led her into a slow, downward spiral of depression and depletion.

Charlotte was a young teenager when her mother tried to take her own life. She was blamed for this by her mother, and no one in her family ever told her it wasn't her fault—except her best friend's parents, who took her in and protected her while her mother was hospitalized. These two adults, and Charlotte's best friend, were the only ones to pour love, courage, hope and joy into her torn-asundered heart. They were her human "saviors" and almost singlehandedly protected Charlotte from a future that could have looked much worse than it does, thanks be to God.

Gratefully and remarkably, Charlotte did well in school academically and socially. Her friends and her studies were lifelines to the greater world of opportunity, health and well-being. She got into her first-choice college and enjoyed those years of her life with great fortitude. She was introduced to the gospel and came to know Jesus in a personal way. This was much different from when she attended church with her family and worried about her behavior and any scolding that would occur when they got home. Now her faith came alive and her love for God increased. Joy entered her heart and the laughter and good times she enjoyed with good friends were life saving. College is also when she met Jason and fell in love.

Jason and Charlotte got married a year after they finished college. Planning the wedding was very stressful with Charlotte's family, but the saving grace was a move more than one thousand miles from her home after the ceremony. Jason came from a very loving family, and his mom quickly lavished love on Charlotte. She smiled and tolerated his mother's affection for about six months but then started to resist it. She also had a hard time with the rest of Jason's family, mostly because they were the polar opposite of her family of origin and they actually loved one another and enjoyed times together. This was confusing for Charlotte. How could this be true?

It took about three years for Charlotte to begin to appreciate Jason's mother and the deep love she had for Charlotte. It was genuine, offered freely and generously, without any expectations or conditions. Jason's mother became Charlotte's most treasured gift in life. Their relationship began to deepen, and Charlotte started to heal from the scars of her dysfunctional and painful childhood. Living far from home and close to Jason's family was the recipe of God's redemption for Charlotte. She grew in her faith, established a new understanding of how God uniquely blessed her with gifts and abilities, trusted Jason's mother in a major way, matured in her own giftedness and relational sensitivities, and became much better prepared for motherhood herself.

Today Charlotte is the mother of four grown children, all of whom are out of the home and building their own lives. They each have spread their wings and are becoming the persons God intends. With an empty nest, Charlotte is now investing in the lives of the next generation. She serves as a mentor for younger mothers learning the ropes of motherhood. She's a transformed woman and serves in her roles as wife, mother, friend, teacher, listener, counselor and leader with a powerful testimony of how God has redeemed every ounce of her pain for his glory. As a leader of young mothers and teacher of young children, she's in the sweet spot of her giftedness and calling. It's such a joy to know Charlotte and to see the delight in her heart and the fruitfulness of her life in Christ. She's blossoming in new ways with each passing year.

LOVE ALWAYS TRUSTS

Charlotte suffered from blatant insecurities, which nearly destroyed her life. If it weren't for her best friend and her friend's parents, Jason and his mom, a faithful counselor and wise mentor, and the Christian community who welcomed her with open arms immediately after their marriage, it's likely Charlotte's story would have turned a much different direction. Instead of growing up in a healthy family system, Charlotte needed to find personal health, spiritual well-being and relational wholeness outside the walls of her family of origin. This is the case for many leaders today who have grown up in environments not at all conducive to personal integrity and vitality. Thankfully for Charlotte and others like her, the body of Christ can be a place where trust is established in heart, soul, mind and strength. Is this not the role of the Christian community for every generation?

To discover a trusting love is to ascertain one of life's most primary values. Trust covers a multitude of mishaps and leads to an ever-deepening experience of genuine affection for the triune God, our only true source of trust. Without trust there is no abundant life.

When the apostle Paul wrote the simple words "love always trusts" his fundamental purpose was to remind the leaders of the Corinthian church to always trust the love of God first and foremost. In so doing, they would be led to live in a trustworthy fashion among the community they were called to lovingly serve and experience fruitfulness in their faithful service to others.

We see a variety of places where Paul seeks to model faithful trustworthiness among the Corinthians leaders who desired to fully trust God. Who else but Paul could pull off being trusted among so many in order to win as many to Christ? He writes, "To the Jews I became a Jew, to win the Jews. To those under the law I became like one under the law (though I myself am not under the law), so as to win those under the law. To those not having the law I became like one not having the law (though I am not free from God's law but am under Christ's law), so as to win those not having the law. To the weak I became weak, to win the weak. I have become all things to all men so that by all possible means I might save some" (1 Corinthians 9:20-22). And all of this was for the sake of the gospel that he might share in its blessings as a faithful, trustworthy representative of Jesus. Paul was trusted by many, and his followers expanded in numbers and deepened in conviction about what it would mean for them to in turn follow Christ. Paul was receivable, trustworthy and compelling in his life, message and ongoing invitation for them to put their trust in God.

Paul was convinced of his call to proclaim the gospel to his generation. He trained as a runner in a race, in order to obtain the prize of eternal joy of seeing others come to a living and eternal faith in Christ. Paul's unbridled trust of the God who loved, redeemed, transformed and commissioned him to this life of service allowed others to see him as a trustworthy leader fit to present a spacious offer of salvation.

In his second letter to the Corinthians, we see a few more examples of this faithful trustworthiness. With an earnest desire to be a "pleasing aroma of Christ" among those who are being saved and those who are perishing, Paul and his band of brothers speak with sincerity and conviction (2 Corinthians 2:14-17). His message is always for the benefit of others; there is no sense of peddling the word of God for profit. Thus he was a trusted voice among the believers and even the unbelievers. He was consistent in his gospel presentation and in his invitation to faithful living for Christ in that pagan, spiritually bankrupt city.

Paul's ministry among the Corinthians was filled with challenges. He endured many a hardship for the sake of Christ:

> In great endurance; in troubles, hardships and distresses; in beatings, imprisonments and riots; in hard work, sleepless nights and hunger; in purity, understanding, patience and kindness; in the Holy Spirit and in sincere love; in truthful speech and in the power of God; with weapons of righteousness in the right hand and in the left; through glory and dishonor, bad report and good report; genuine, yet regarded as impostors; known, yet regarded as

unknown; dying, and yet we live on; beaten, and yet not killed; sorrowful, yet always rejoicing; poor, yet making many rich; having nothing, and yet possessing everything. (2 Corinthians 6:4-10)

His willingness to suffer for others made his message all the more palatable and worthy of a dedicated following.

Why? Because his motivation was to open wide his heart to them in order that they would open wide their hearts to God (2 Corinthians 6:11-13). What a beautiful testimony of the gift of trust freely and generously offered that, when graciously and trustingly received, produces life-changing results. With the humility and gentleness of Christ (2 Corinthians 10:10), Paul pleads for their faithful response. Trusting him and his message will lead them out of their dysfunction and into full fellowship with the God who sent Paul, the same God who offers himself to each and every one of them in Christ.

Therefore, "let him who boasts boast in the Lord. For it is not the one who commends himself who is approved, but the one whom the Lord commends" (2 Corinthians 10:17-18). The trust Paul earns among them comes from the deep well of trust he has in God. He felt deeply about that which he knew theologically and experientially of the God who sent him as a representative of Christ to the spiritually tormented and relationally tattered city of Corinth. His legacy continues to live on in our hearts today.

INVITATION TO RESTORE TRUST AND EMBRACE FAITHFULNESS

Rueben Job, one of the most highly esteemed and trusted spiritual mentors of our generation (a recently deceased Methodist bishop, author and compiler of several guides to prayer and other spiritual formation resources), just months before his death, offered a simple quote that has become cemented in my soul. On the verge of death's door, confined to hospice care, living with a small percentage of his heart functioning, not knowing if he would awake each new morning after a night of sleep, he shared six simple words that have subsequently altered my spiritual life: "All of life is about trust."

All of life? Simply about trust? As I sat with this phrase, arrested by its power, touched by its poignancy, I had little to offer in rebuttal. All of life is indeed about learning how to trust God. We can't be trusted fully; we will undoubtedly and inevitably breach trust somewhere along the journey of life. Others we know will threaten or dismantle our trust in them. But one thing remains constant and trustworthy: the God of trustworthy love will never walk away, never turn his back and never neglect his most basic offering to humankind since the dawn of time. If we attend to his presence, hear his voice, listen for his truth, submit to his authority and live for his kingdom, we too will know with certainty what it means to trust God. When that trust is securely planted in our hearts and souls, we will in turn be entrusted with the gospel and invited daily to live as a trustworthy representative of Christ.

But none of this is possible in our own strength. We can't trust, but in God. When we seek to carry the concerns of this life with our own power, we will eventually tire. However, when we discover the God of love who empowers us by his Spirit with the ability to trust, we can claim that gift as our own and, ultimately, lean fully into living a life of trusting love and faithfulness.

Love (always) trusts in times of temptation, trial, testing and tribulation. Trust comes to fruition in our hearts and lives only when we lean into God's loving, trustworthy arms. On the heels of Jesus' baptism, God declares his love for his beloved Son, in whom he is well pleased, and a dove descends as a sign of God's Spirit and blessing. Immediately thereafter (Luke 4), Jesus is led by the Spirit into the desert where he enters a forty-day season of temptation. His full allegiance for his Father is tested under the devil's scrutiny. On three dramatic occasions, Jesus faces off with significant temptation. The devil's challenges are stark: "Tell this stone to become bread"; "If you worship me, it will all be yours" and "If you are the Son of God, throw yourself down from here." Jesus responds to each of them with directives from the Word (all are quotes from Deuteronomy): "Man does not live on bread alone"; "Worship the Lord your God and serve him only" and "Do not put the Lord your God to the test" (Luke 4:3-9, 12).

The Scriptures are filled with trust-building examples. When the truth of God's Word is firmly planted in our hearts, then no matter the trial or temptation, we can trust God in its midst. Jesus survived those forty wilderness days, and when he re-entered the synagogue he proclaimed his mission to all who were in earshot. Rather than hindering him, the testing he endured catapulted him into the fulfillment of his God-ordained life of witness and service to all.

In this life there will be trouble. In leadership, among any and all people groups, within any number of missional tasks, there will be testing in the form of trials and temptations. It's inevitable. It's the fodder of transformation. Therefore, trusting in God's love amid times of testing and tribulation will deepen our affection for God's unfailing trustworthiness.

Love (always) trusts in times of heartache and disappointment. In addition to the trials, testing and temptations of life, there will be many times when our unmet expectations lead to heartache and disappointment. The Scriptures are replete with examples of this, from the story of creation until the day of eternal consummation and exaltation. Jesus himself experienced many such disappointments. In the Garden of Gethsemane, on the verge of his death, he asks his disciples to pray with him through the watches of the night. Instead, they fall fast asleep and miss this opportunity to serve their Lord. At his darkest hour, one of his disciples betrays him, another disowns him, still others call out for his arrest, humiliation and crucifixion. All of this is to be expected of a fallen and confused humanity. But as we read the text we hope for something more, especially from his closest friends and followers. Jesus' heartache is overcome by the Father's presence and protection during his darkest moments. In turn, we too can trust the Father's presence and protection in our darkest hours or seasons of life.

If it's true that unrealistic expectations can lead us to greater disappointment, then it's healthy for us to monitor our expectations and keep them appropriately sized. If we err on the side of heightened expectations, we may inspire others to reach beyond themselves to God's greater desires, but we may instead be setting ourselves up for even deeper disappointment. Most realistic expectations will result in great contentment for all as we learn how to live within God's best for us. Living lovingly, freely and with trust is always the best posture. As leaders, we need to acknowledge the ripple effects of unusually high expectations and the potential net negative effect they can create in our hearts and among those we serve. And we must remember there is no disappointment in life where God isn't deeper still, fully present to protect you and provide for you, often far greater than you could ever ask, dream or imagine.

Love (always) trusts in times of riches, plenty and abundance. Not only in times of scarcity but also in seasons of abundance, we need to remain in a trusting posture. When the early church was in their season of Pentecost, the fullness of the Spirit was evident in every sphere of their shared life. As a result, they experienced unity in worship, witness and work. They rejoiced in the many who were coming to faith in Christ. There was no need beyond what could be met by the community. The Lord's blessing was clearly apparent. The Spirit was moving powerfully in their midst. No one could refute the results (read Acts 2–4 for all the rich details).

Barnabas was known among the early church as a man of integrity, wisdom and godliness. He sold a property he owned, brought the full price received and laid the money at the apostles' feet to be used for the furthering of Christ's kingdom on earth. One can only imagine the joy this sparked within that burgeoning faith community. Barnabas's complete generosity was a testimony to his trustworthiness as a leader in the church. This generous man of faith testified that trusting God in times of plenty would reap great fruit for generations to come. No one could refute the evidence of Barnabas's trusting lifestyle, and the church was blessed abundantly.

Trust God. Trust others. Trust yourself. When trust breaks down, do everything possible to rebuild and restore it. Without trust there is no meaningful life. To become trustworthy is to realize that trust itself is the mortar that keeps the structure of life intact. Love always trusts. A trusting soul is one that's entrusted with that which is bigger than us. With whom and toward what end are you entrusted to love in this life?

A trustworthy person embodies several noteworthy traits. To begin with, our character is to embody *loyalty, truthfulness* and *genuine promise keeping*. Then, our lifestyle is to be marked with *integrity*, the conjoining of heart, voice, conviction, empathic communication, follow through and accountability. We courageously *persevere* toward the goal of being cooperative and just, standing up for that which is right in the eyes of God. We are *content* and *humble*, which is best expressed freely, genuinely, rather instinctively and always generously as an outflow of the faithfulness of God. Humility is also expressed in our deeply contented sense of our truest self, as defined so beautifully by God. In other words, a life of trustworthiness looks a lot like Jesus himself, who was the complete embodiment of these characteristics—and serves as our example to emulate.

Life is indeed all about trust. Love always trusts.

Spiritual Leadership Audit

Restoring Your Trustworthy Faithfulness

In order for love to always trust, we need to understand what it means to live under the daily, loving empowerment of the Holy Spirit. To consider a life of trust separated from the work of God's Spirit is impossible. We simply can't love in a trusting way without the Spirit. That's why it's imperative for us as leaders to consider the ways we've experienced trust being broken, abused, neglected or assumed. In some cases we were the primary cause, and in many other circumstances we were victims of breaches of trust created by others.

Regardless of the source, it's incredibly life-giving to be given the opportunity to repair broken trust and move, with love, toward restitution and reconciliation. Sometimes our prayerful efforts will reap marvelous fruit; other times we will simply have to wait and hold fast to a deep trust in God no matter the results. Yet if you believe that love always trusts, then let me encourage you to enter this reflection with a sense of joyful anticipation and receive from the Lord his trustworthiness, allowing him to form you more and more into a trustworthy leader.

Confess your brokenness: Naming your brokenness and owning it as a present reality.

- In what way(s) have you found yourself lacking trust in others, or absent of trustworthiness toward or from others, most recently?

- Consider prayerfully the details of this experience and recount them here.

Rest and trust in God's abiding presence and peace: Seeking God's trusting love to be revealed and released from within your soul.

- *Hopeful in Scripture*: Read the account of Jesus' baptism and blessing and the temptation in the desert wilderness that follows (Luke 3–4). What do you notice about the importance of Jesus' blessing ("You are my Son, whom I love; with you I am well pleased") in contrast to the temptations he endured in the desert?

- *Faithful in prayer*: Ask the Lord for clarity about your greatest temptations. How should you handle them in the future?

- *Thankful in reflection*: Now notice Jesus' return to the synagogue and pronouncement of his mission to all who are present (Luke 5). What does your mission-focused "scroll" look like, and how will God's trusting love be revealed and released through you in the coming days?

Invite God to redeem your brokenness: Restoring God's trustworthy love in you.

- In what circumstances or among what relationships are you most challenged as a leader today? What would it look like for you to hold them with greater and more intentional open-handedness rather than with a clinging desire to control?

- The posture of trust will always be open—open arms, open hands, open ears, open eyes, open heart. How will you position yourself accordingly when you face times of temptation, disappointment and also abundance?

- "All of life is about trust." Commit these six words to memory. Consider ways to document or creatively display these words somewhere visible to remind you of their poignancy. I guarantee they will change your life!

- eleven -

When Hope Waxes and Wanes

Love always hopes

MY FRIEND MIKE IS MORE FAMILIAR than he wishes with the
suffering and debilitation that's caused by heart-wrenching
despair. His father left the family when he was very young. He
struggled to survive with the remaining members of the family
and endured the challenges of a broken home.

As a young adult, he married the love of his life, fathered four
children with her, only to learn years later that she never really
loved him. She kicked him out of the house with two garbage
bags full of his life possessions. She remarried and moved with
the children two thousand miles away. He was forlorn, forgotten,
broke and broken.

One day on a rather perfunctory trip to the dump, he found a
book on the shelf in the "still good" shed (a section in the dump
where one man's trash is another man's treasure), a biography
about the late William Booth, founder of the Salvation Army. He
read the book from cover to cover and within a week was on the
doorstep of the local Salvation Army center. His only hope was

that he wouldn't be turned away. Indeed, he was received in love and miraculously saved.

Not only did the Salvation Army officers on duty welcome Mike with open arms that day, they also ushered him graciously and generously into their lives. They introduced him to the radical and redemptive love of Christ, which he willingly accepted with joy. They included him in their broken but redeemed community of faith, and he's never been the same since.

Today Mike is an officer in the Salvation Army. He's remarried to a wonderful woman who is a Salvation Army Captain. Together they are mending their lives and serving one of the largest corps of the northeast United States. Mike has since restored his relationships with his children and is on amiable terms with his former wife. He's on his way to significant leadership in the Salvation Army, following in the footsteps and upholding the amazing legacy of his hero, the late William Booth.

It's inspiring to sit and listen to Mike as he freely shares the details of his journey, finding strength in weakness, claiming hope from despair and rediscovering wholeness out of his brokenness. He describes his walk with God in intimate fashion, and he ascribes times of silence, solitude and prayerful reflection as his "beautiful broken place" where God is restoring and renewing him from the inside out. Without such soul care and Spirit-empowered formation, he's not sure where he'd be today. His ability to receive and reflect on the experiences of his life is what brings him into deeper fellowship with God. His life is robust, delightful, humble, redeemed and, very simply, beautiful.

During a recent "red kettle" campaign in the frenzy of the Christmas season, one of Mike's volunteers returned his kettle, ready for the contents to be counted up at the end of his shift. He had been in a nearby train station ringing his bell and thereby inviting those who were passing by to make a contribution. Little did he know at the time that a woman had dropped a lightly folded plastic bag in his kettle. It sat among the bills and loose change deposited by many others that afternoon and evening.

When Mike and his team were counting up the proceeds from the kettles delivered to the corps that evening, they were surprised to discover the plastic bag. Contained within was a short handwritten note and two gold rings; one was a woman's wedding band and the other a diamond engagement ring. The note contained a simple request, "To honor the memory of my late husband, I'm hoping there's someone out there who made lots of money this year and will buy the rings for ten times their worth. After all, there's no price on love or the sentimental value of the rings. But money will help the kids." The donor knew that her husband always had a giving spirit—especially at Christmas, and the gift would be in good hands buying toys for needy children by the reputable Salvation Army.

The plastic bag also included a description of the rings and their assessed value, provided by a local jeweler and dated several years prior, obviously at the original date of purchase. Original value of the rings: $1,850. The story caught the interest of all the local news media outlets, and within days there were pledges made by persons of means who were willing to receive the rings in return for a hefty donation to the Salvation Army.

As the days progressed, and more and more people expressed interest, the highest amount pledged was $21,000—more than ten times the original purchase price. And, to the surprise of all, the person with the premier bid also wanted the Salvation Army to try and track down the donor of the rings . . . and return the rings, assuming the woman would appreciate keeping them for sentimental reasons. The giver, a widow, placed no conditions on the donation; it was simply offered with no strings (or rings!) attached. The story of the donated rings was inspiration and motivation enough.

Two days before Christmas "the tale of two widows" came to a happy ending. The rings were reunited with their original owner in an emotional private meeting between the two women. Mike and his wife were the only others present. Mike had delight in his heart and tears in his eyes when recounting the reunion, "Both of these women are heroes to me. This is the true meaning of Christmas." Both agreed that spending the holiday season without their husbands was difficult, but that their spirits were buoyed by each other's act of generosity. "You've made my Christmas," the second donor told the first. "You've made mine," the ring donor replied.

To hear Mike share his story with a mile-wide grin on his face is pure joy. Here's a man of God in a leadership role by the grace of God, dispensing the gospel of Christ both tangibly and intangibly to all in his care. His once despairing life is now fully devoted to sharing the hope-filled gospel of love to a city and its children in need. The Salvation Army daily serves a great cause, continually replacing despair with hope.

LOVE ALWAYS HOPES

Hope is a warm blanket that covers the soul. It provides the much-needed confidence for us that life is held more securely when repeatedly placed into the palms of God's loving hands. Hope births freedom deep within, buoys the spirit and energizes the heart. Hope is endless and yet immediate, tireless and yet restful, knowing and yet innocent. It's easy to say but difficult to explain. One either has it or not; it can't be forced or transplanted. It can, however, come alive in what appears to be a dormant life. Hope is one of the most generous gifts we can offer to one another, for seeds of hope will always reap a faithful harvest in the soul.

When the apostle Paul lived and served among the Corinthians, he poured hope into their hearts continuously. He was tireless in his efforts, focused on kingdom outcomes in and through their shared community of faith. Even though he was determined to identify the issues that needed to be addressed for the sake of the Corinthians' health and vitality, his messages were filled with hope and courageous confidence in Christ. Those who had ears to hear and a heart willing to respond to his leadership experienced the most meaningful life change.

What did the Corinthians do in return as an expression of gratitude for Paul's message of hope? The most tangible response we know of came in the form of the "collection"—their gifts and offerings. Their gifts were the outward expression of the inward transformation the gospel had produced deep within their heart and soul. Paul introduces this in 1 Corinthians 16:1-4 when he asks them to set aside a sum of money, in keeping with their income, so that gifts can be given for those who are heading to serve in Jerusalem.

Then, in 2 Corinthians 8 and 9, Paul continues to encourage and affirm their generosity. He shares with them the liberality and fruitfulness of the Macedonian churches, whose "overflowing joy and their extreme poverty welled up in rich generosity" (8:2) out of a severe trial. He tells the Corinthians how these believers gave as much as they were able, and even beyond their ability, entirely on their own. Then he urges them: "Just as you excel in everything—in faith, in speech, in knowledge, in complete earnestness and in your love for us—see that you also excel in this grace of giving" (8:7). And his challenge is not a command, but is offered "to test the sincerity of your love" (8:8). He reminds them that the prior year they were the first to give, and to desire to give, and then exhorts them to "finish the work, so that your eager willingness to do it may be matched by your completion of it, according to your means. . . . Their plenty will supply what you need" (8:11, 14). Oh the eternal blessings of generosity—always for hope's sake. Paul's offering of his very life and teaching was filled with hope. The church's gifts and offerings in return, given out of a heart of gratitude, kept hope alive and furthered the gospel in their generation.

Paul's continual reminder to sow generously is amplified in chapter 9:

> Remember this: Whoever sows sparingly will also reap sparingly, and whoever sows generously will also reap generously. Each man should give what he has decided in his heart to give, not reluctantly or under compulsion, for God loves a cheerful giver. And God is able to make all grace abound to you, so that in all things at all times, having all that you need, you will abound in every good work. (2 Corinthians 9:6-8)

Again we see the fruitful blessings of generosity—gifts of hope planted in one heart after another.

A loving hope is a generous hope. Seeds of both reap a lavish harvest for all. Without hope and generosity, the gospel and life itself are thwarted.

> Now he who supplies seed to the sower and bread for food will also supply and increase your store of seed and will enlarge the harvest of your righteousness. You will be made rich in every way so that you can be generous on every occasion, and through us your generosity will result in thanksgiving to God. . . .
>
> Because of the service by which you have proved yourselves, men will praise God for the obedience that accom-

panies your confession of the gospel of Christ, and for your
generosity in sharing with them and with everyone else.
And in their prayers for you their hearts will go out to you,
because of the surpassing grace God has given you. Thanks
be to God for his indescribable gift! (2 Corinthians 9:10-15)

All of Paul's teaching about generosity speaks of the truth that
where our treasure is stored, there will be our hearts also.
These words from the lips of Jesus are transmuted by Paul to
his generation, specifically the church in Corinth. As a leader
of a Christian nonprofit organization that depends on the generosity of God's faithful ones, I can attest to the hope in my
heart that balloons inside me as gifts are offered in love. God
indeed loves generosity, for it is a tangible reflection of his
hope for the world. When we give of ourselves and our
resources, we plant seeds of hope that bring forth eternal hope
in the hearts of others.

Those who responded to the hope of Christ in Paul's message
were the ones who experienced abundant life and rose above
their circumstances with hope planted deeply in their hearts.
Wouldn't it be marvelous if the Christian community of our day
would harken to his voice, heed his warnings, generously give of
itself and receive his words of hope? Hope in the heart breeds
generosity unmeasured, and generosity—in all forms—keeps
the gospel of hope alive for all eternity.

INVITATION TO EMBRACE DESPAIR
AND RESTORE HOPEFUL CONFIDENCE IN GOD

For leaders and followers, despair at one level or another is inevitable. We cannot avoid the invariable despair that comes from
everyday life, especially when hard times are accumulated over
months, years, seasons or even a lifetime. What contributes to

any tendency you may have to lean toward despair, the root of
which is fear?

We despair for any number of reasons. We lose hope and
despair when hurtful words are spoken or actions expressed to
us from those with whom we are in relationship. *Relational
despair* can be manifest in marriage and family life, in friendship circles, and among professional colleagues in marketplace
and ministry. When we hurt in the relational sphere of life,
through an affair, divorce, death, separation, alienation, abuse,
neglect or any other form of relational disturbance, we can enter
into despair when those challenges are left dangling or unre-
solved. Because relationships are so complex today, to unravel
the hurt-filled knots takes time and effort, and sometimes even
requires the services of counselors, pastors or spiritual mentors.
Despair in our relationships can often be debilitating for all
other aspects of life and service to others.

We despair when we suffer from *unattended heartache* of our
past or present experiences. Heartache comes from various
sources, in all shapes and sizes, and is indiscriminate in its
release. We suffer heartache in life's disappointments. We may
have been raised in dysfunctional families that didn't know any
way other than to abuse, neglect or judge harshly. We may have
been exposed to sinful tendencies that have led to addictive
traits and altered our personalities. We may not be able to distinguish truth from lies, having been informed mostly by those
who can't handle truth telling. We may have chemical imbal-
ances to moderate with medication. Any one of these situations,
and thousands more, can lead to anxiety, sadness and/or depression. The end result understandably is despair.

We also despair when we are *facing loss*. Loss looks different
according to one's circumstance. Loss of life is the most notable,
especially when that life is someone dear to us: a family member,

friend, mentor, colleague or even a pet. But we can also face the loss of our job or house or neighborhood. Loss can come as a result of divorce, sickness or natural disaster. It may be a loss of a season of life (e.g., children moving out of the nest) or the loss of a dream or aspiration for our future (or the future of a loved one). It may be loss of hearing or memory that comes as a result of illness or with the aging process. Or the loss may be of a special friendship that's gone awry. No matter the loss, we need to learn how to grieve it appropriately. To do so, we must recognize the commonly noted five stages of grief espoused by Elisabeth Kübler-Ross in *On Death and Dying*: denial, anger, bargaining, depression and acceptance. To embrace our despair in this way will ultimately lead us into both acceptance and renewed hope.

Whenever we are tempted to despair, we need to remember to place a stake in the ground that confirms our confidence, trust and hope in God alone. We must refuse despair's entry at the doorpost of our hearts whenever possible. Despair wreaks havoc on our walk with the living God who wants us to instead relish the gift of hope always being offered to us in Christ Jesus. As Paul reminded the Corinthians, "We have this treasure in jars of clay to show that this all-surpassing power is from God and not from us. We are hard pressed on every side, but not crushed; perplexed, but not in despair; persecuted, but not abandoned; struck down, but not destroyed. We always carry around in our body the death of Jesus, so that the life of Jesus may also be revealed in our body. . . . Therefore we do not lose heart" (2 Corinthians 4:7-10, 16). Instead of despairing of life's very perplexing realities, especially in complex leadership situations, we are to be people who are brimming with the fullness of hope that comes from Jesus Christ. We must not lose heart.

If we are to ever really understand how love always hopes, we need to rely on the richness of hope that God desires for us. The key is to keep hope alive in our own hearts and then remain open to how God may wish for us to keep hope alive in the hearts of others. We must remember at all times that hope is one of the best gifts we can both receive from God and offer graciously to others in his behalf.

We keep hope alive by believing in God. On a recent Soul Sabbath (a day-long silence and solitude prayer retreat) a participant said he was desirous of "feeling what we know." It's one thing to have a head full of knowledge about God, but belief in God must go deeper. Full belief takes that which is known and plants it in the heart. When belief resides in its appropriate place within, we can't help but feel God's presence, taste and see that he is good, and even touch the hem of his garment as we reach out for more and more of him. When we hunger and thirst for the living God, he never disappoints or withholds his presence from us.

We keep hope alive by resting in God. The psalmist David begins Psalm 62 with seven words that will change your life: "My soul finds rest in God alone." The only way hope is kept alive is through our ability to rest fully in the loving embrace of God. When we pursue such rest elsewhere, we will inevitably be disappointed. We can't find complete rest in our relationships; people will ultimately disappoint us. We can't find total rest in our vocations; our work can't fully satisfy our deepest longings. We can't find certain rest in our world; what the culture offers is rarely good for the soul. We can't find eternal rest in our resources; our money, possessions, and even our innate abilities and aptitudes will never satisfy. We can only find hope by resting in God.

We keep hope alive by trusting in God. Trusting in God is the only way we will fully embrace hope. No matter what life may offer, God is there to be trusted. His wisdom is higher than any person's intellect. His power is greater than any force we can muster up ourselves or any power issued from our world. His presence is everywhere, and since there is no place we can hide from him, the Lord will be with us at all times. Since "all of life is about trust" we can discover the richness of hope by trusting implicitly in God. Giving all that we are or have in this life generously back to God is the best place to begin.

We keep hope alive by hoping in God. "'For I know the plans I have for you,' declares the LORD, 'plans to prosper you and not to harm you, plans to give you hope and a future. Then you will call upon me and come and pray to me, and I will listen to you. You will seek me and find me when you seek me with all your heart'" (Jeremiah 29:11-13). Hoping in God is what keeps hope alive. When we know with depth and certainty that our lives are really his, we hope for a future that's brighter and more promising than the present. God pledged to his people of old and to his disciples today that as we seek him with all our heart we will find him. As we call on him and pray to him, God loves to listen. We are his beloved ones, and his future for us is filled with hope.

By facing the full depth of our despair—running toward and not away from it—and then praying toward hopefulness, we will truly discover what it means to love always with hope.

Spiritual Leadership Audit

Restoring Your Hope

As it was with the Corinthian church, so it is today: hope springs eternal when it's preceded and surrounded with gratitude and generosity. Searching for hope? It's often found through our own thankfulness and in giving ourselves away. Even when we are in a place of despair, it's good for us to give thanks for the hardships of life that may be feeding the despair. When we embrace despair in all its fullness and unlock the door of our despairing and sometimes despondent hearts, we will find that God is always present, accompanying us every step of the way.

Regardless of what's feeding a sense of hopelessness in or around you, can you believe God for the hope that he longs for you to abundantly experience? Let the blanket of hope envelop your heart today. Receive the generous love of God from the arms and voice and gifts of the people of God. May the hope of Christ fill you to overflowing in the dark hours of the night and in the brightness of each new day. And may you be true to your calling as beacons and bearers of hope to all who cross your path.

Confess your brokenness: Naming your brokenness and owning it as a present reality.

- In what way(s) have you found yourself despairing, or experienced others despairing, most recently?

- Consider prayerfully the details of this experience and recount them here.

Rest and trust in God's abiding presence and peace: Seeking God's hopefulness to be revealed and released from within your soul.

- *Hopeful in Scripture*: Read both Romans 5:2-5 and 2 Corinthians 4:16-18. What do they have in common with one another?

- *Faithful in prayer*: In what way(s) do you find yourself despairing of hope? Ask the Lord to reveal any tendencies toward despair that you might need to attend to specifically.

- *Thankful in reflection*: If you were to embrace your particular propensity to despair, what would that look like? Are you willing to get close to it, recognize its source, and deal with it prayerfully, professionally and/or personally?

Invite God to redeem your brokenness: Restoring God's loving hope in you. In the beautiful story of the sinful woman sitting at the feet of Jesus in Luke 7:36-50, we see her weeping tears, wiping perfume and worshiping Jesus in ways that were offensive to Simon the Pharisee and the onlookers who gathered in that household. If we put our ears as close as possible to this text, we almost hear her words of grace ("I'm sorry"), gratitude ("thank you") and generosity ("I love you").

- Grace—invite God to redeem your despair; offer words of confession in your prayer.

- Gratitude—express heartfelt thankfulness to God for meeting you in your despair and offering words of hope from his Word.

- Generosity—with open hands, consider who in your sphere of influence needs to be offered some seeds of hope, and offer them lovingly, either tangibly or intangibly, in Jesus' name.

- twelve -

No Pain Is Ever Wasted

Love always perseveres and never fails

SHIRLEY CAME TO HER LEADERSHIP ROLE with a contagious enthusiasm. The presentations she made to the board that hired her seemed quite promising. Her résumé was impressive, and the teams she had previously built were delighted to follow her charming charisma. So, when the twenty-five-year-old organization hired Shirley, their first female CEO, the mood among the staff, board and constituency was at its highest in more than a decade.

Considered one of the top leaders under thirty-five in the nation, Shirley was on the rise. She was a significant voice among her female CEO peers. She was an excellent public speaker who readily captivated the audiences she addressed. She had a supportive husband and two young children who were cared for daily by their grandmother, Shirley's mother-in-law. Shirley's family photo added a nice touch to the organization's promotional material.

Having previously served on the board of this national ministry, Shirley was familiar with some of the daunting

challenges ahead of her. There had been two previous execu-
tives in her role who had unsuccessfully followed a much-
beloved and long-term predecessor, the founder, who had
made a reputation for himself as a true pioneer. Shirley knew
that even though there had been two others before her, everyone would be comparing her tenure with the man who put
them on the map over twenty years ago. Further, he was still
on the team as an honorary ex-officio member of the board,
generally behind the scenes but very present at select times.
She was determined to treat his legacy with appropriate gratitude.

The three biggest issues for Shirley to deal with included (1)
refining their missional focus; (2) rebuilding trust among their
various constituents; and (3) establishing a compelling strategic
agenda for the future. For nearly ten years, this organization had
floundered along without any sense of a compelling agenda for
the present, never mind the future. Her predecessors had made
some poor decisions that offended several key leaders but ironically had galvanized the staff (or so it was perceived). By the time
Shirley was hired, no one had a clear sense for where they were
heading and whether it was time to instead close the doors and
call it a day.

Shirley believed in the historical mission of the group she was
now called to lead. Her father had been a key player nearly two
decades prior to her assuming this new role. He was a "legend"
of sorts, having worked with the founder, with whom he shared
a deep friendship and camaraderie. Shirley wanted to uphold
their legacy. One of the first things she did in her tenure was
spend a full day with her dad and the founder. She learned so
much about the history of the organization and recognized with
greater clarity how it had wandered away from its original mission. She was off to a great start.

However, what transpired after only three months on the job came as a complete surprise. One Monday morning after a long week on the road, Shirley entered her office and found three envelopes on her desk. They were resignation letters from three of her top staff members: her vice president of finance, the vice president of special programs and her executive assistant. Her immediate assumption was that they were obviously in collusion with one another, and she wanted to get to the bottom of this right away. So she asked each person to come and explain their respective letter. She listened intently and by the end of the morning had accepted all three resignations. There didn't seem to be anything venomous about their withdrawals, even though two of them were headed to the same organization and the third was simply retiring.

This was a huge hit on Shirley's leadership. She never suspected that personnel issues would become her focus so early on. What was becoming clear to her, however, is that her two previous leaders had nearly exhausted the staff. What others perceived as a strong team had actually developed into a multi-silo approach—each department was independent of the others. The workload and expectations continued to rise, and the atmosphere was becoming toxic. The interim leadership team had done everything possible to keep the ship afloat, but by the time Shirley came on board, with her winsome enthusiasm for the way forward, the team around her simply didn't have the energy to try yet another new approach. They all lived in a city where other ministries were present, and the job market was ripe for them to make changes.

Within another three months, two more key staff resigned and left holes for Shirley to fill. Still, she stepped to the plate and offered her best work to recruit and hire people that would fit the current needs of the organization. Her renewed vision was becoming clearer as the weeks progressed, and she had the full support of the board to build her team as she so desired. But after a very difficult first year at the helm, she entered the annual meeting exhausted from the staffing changes and didn't have much energy for her strategic presentations.

The annual meeting was actually pretty chaotic, mostly because the newness of Shirley's presence had waned, the staff who had previously organized these meetings were gone, and many loose ends became quite obvious. The key board members present a year earlier were not there, for various reasons, and their presence was missed. The team designated to give update reports from the field was not as informed as they needed to be. Even Shirley's CEO report fell flat. The board members gathered were a bit discouraged and became quickly disillusioned with Shirley's leadership. There was a call from the floor for a closed meeting, which meant Shirley and the staff would not be present.

Thankfully for all concerned, Shirley's spiritual mentor (also a board member) was present in the room when Shirley was making her CEO report. She noticed Shirley's exhaustion and approached her lovingly after the meeting was over. Shirley admitted to her that she was indeed very tired, that she had been working way too hard. She wept in her mentor's arms as she poured out her heart. When the board met privately in executive session, they discussed Shirley's leadership, the staff who had left over the past year, and the need to stay the course and not give up. Thankfully, they were of one mind and chose to persevere.

What transpired in the following months became a great example for others to emulate. Shirley was recommissioned to serve in her role, with new parameters in place to ensure her health and well-being, which in turn would positively affect the entire board, staff, field team and wider constituency. They all went back to the basics, took their founder off the pedestal they had placed him on, and humbly confessed to God and one another the need to be pliable in God's hands. Shirley was their leader and deserved their full support moving forward.

Within a few short months, the organization found its equilibrium once more. Shirley was living a much healthier lifestyle, spending more time with her family and taking better care of herself physically, emotionally and spiritually. She slowly added quality members to her leadership team and rebuilt trust among the volunteer field staff who oversaw key programs. Funding picked up once more, excellent resources were created, and the much-needed infrastructure was rebuilt. The organization was once again heading in the right direction.

LOVE PERSEVERES, NEVER FAILS OR ENDS

Courage or cowardice: that's the choice. To love with perseverance requires the former and is an offense to the latter. Cowards live behind a preserved persona, and the courageous are willing to persevere without such pretense. The apostle Paul confronts the Corinthian church mostly because of their cowardice in not living faithfully, in Christ-honoring ways and in accordance with the gospel they are called to proclaim. They had collapsed many of the standards they were taught to adhere to and instead allowed the culture to inform their way of being and living.

Every step of the way, Paul loves the church in Corinth with a courageous and persevering love. He's tireless in his approach, and he has a terrific handle on the issues at hand. He's a leader's leader in so many ways, and in his two letters to the Corinthians he shows a holy boldness unparalleled in many leadership circles then and now. He was willing to go wherever necessary in order to bring the church back to its intended focus: loving God and serving others with gladness and singleness of heart.

It took someone courageous and persevering to pull off Paul's calling.

To persevere in love is not an easy undertaking, nor is it for the faint of heart. However, with the empowerment of the Spirit, even the most timid and tame can rise above their personal challenges and courageously go where they may never have gone before. When that happens, a truly great leader rises to the occasion and calls forth love and faithfulness from followers who are eager to know the way. Paul's relentless perseverance amidst incredible obstacles is admirable in many ways. To read the books of 1 and 2 Corinthians through this lens of leadership is astonishing, to say the least.

Where would we be without love to guide, protect and sustain us? Love not only perseveres; it never fails or fades or falls away, unlike other gifts like prophecies, which will cease; and tongues, which will be stilled; and knowledge, which will pass away (1 Corinthians 13:8). Even graces like faith and hope will never be preferred over love (1 Corinthians 13:13). And although we can see love only in a childish, unclear reflection here on earth (1 Corinthians 13:9-12), the love of God not only lasts forever but also is our guiding light during our life on earth. The unceasing nature of God's love defines and defends us until we are ushered into eternity to experience nothing but love. In heaven we will perfectly and maturely love God and one another, but until then we only see it in a mirror dimly lit.

The apostle Paul gives voice to the never-ending, all-sufficient love of God in virtually every book he wrote and through every encounter he experienced as he built up the church. He sustained many heartaches, injuries and setbacks that could have pulled him out of the game. If it were not for the love of God, Paul would have been a paralyzed failure. His own sinfulness would have gotten in the way of the will of God.

But over and over again God kept him, directed him and provided for him all that he would need. God's love was his fortress, his strength, his deliverer, his hope, his trust and his leader, every step of the way.

In all of his afflictions, Paul was granted victory in Christ. And he praised the Lord within each of his sufferings:

> Praise be to the God and Father of our Lord Jesus Christ, the Father of compassion and the God of all comfort, who comforts us in all our troubles, so that we can comfort those in any trouble with the comfort we ourselves have received from God. For just as the sufferings of Christ flow over into our lives, so also through Christ our comfort overflows . . . We suffered . . . far beyond our ability to endure . . . that we might not rely on ourselves but on God. . . . He will deliver us. On him we have set our hope that . . . many will give thanks on our behalf for the gracious favor granted us in answer to the prayers of many. (2 Corinthians 1:3-5, 8-11)

The unfailing love of God sustained Paul and his companions. The comfort and compassion of God was his bulwark never failing. His boasting was not of himself but of the surpassing greatness and generosity of God. It was love that guided his heart, and it was the steadfast love and mercy of God that remained his central message to each of the churches he formed and fed in love. In love he recognized how God used the churches for his purposes, so that he could travel from city to city without any "letters of recommendation" (2 Corinthians 3:1) for his leadership. Instead, and in typical Paul fashion, he would say of them, "You yourselves are our letter, written on our hearts, known and read by everybody. You show that you are a letter from Christ, the result of our ministry, written not with ink but with the Spirit of the living God, not on tablets of stone but on tablets of human hearts" (2 Corinthians 3:2-3).

The ripple effects of love became evident in the churches Paul founded, led and served so faithfully. Because of Paul's dramatic conversion to Christ, he was sincerely motivated to present the gospel of Christ to as many as possible, as far away as possible. His missionary journeys were efficacious and victorious in so many ways. Because of the unconditional love of Christ that he presented to his beloved ones, his words, lifestyle and ministry were living demonstrations of his faithfulness. For Paul, it was true: love never fails, it never ends, it never quits, it never ceases to reign supreme. "My love to all of you in Christ Jesus" (1 Corinthians 16:24) was his closing line of affection over and over again.

Paul's words to the church in Corinth are reminiscent of the words of Jeremiah as recorded for us in Lamentations 3:19-24:

> I remember my affliction and my wandering,
> the bitterness and the gall.
> I well remember them,
> and my soul is downcast within me.
> Yet this I call to mind
> and therefore I have hope:
>
> Because of the LORD's great love we are not consumed,
> for his compassions never fail.
> They are new every morning;
> great is your faithfulness.
> I say to myself, "The LORD is my portion;
> therefore I will wait for him."

Great words of great leaders inspire love for God and sacrificial service to others. Always.

Love perseveres. Love never ends. Love never fails. Love never fades. Love never becomes obsolete. Love never dies. These are simple yet profound words that will always sustain, both in times of triumph and in times of trouble.

INVITATION TO PERSEVERANCE IN THE FACE OF FEAR

A coward lives in fear. When fear has a tight grasp on the heart of a leader, there is a feeling of imprisonment within. It's exhibited in an excessive self-concern that overrides any sense of doing or saying the right thing. The failures of a coward can become destructive to others. A cowardly leader has a weak sense of self and an even weaker following.

On the other hand, courage is perseverance in the face of fear. Courageous leaders come head to head in combat against their fears. Courage that's planted deep in the heart perseveres in spite of obstacles. It's being willing to say and do the right thing regardless of the mental or physical pain required. Never skirting fear or taking the easy route, a courageous person is prepared to vault over the highest bar of virtue in order to attain the goal. For the Christian leader, courage is found not in the human strength required to vault but in the Spirit's power that comes alive in the decision to persevere. Courage is then lived out in an active trust in God to provide the fortitude and strength to overcome all odds and to prayerfully persevere.

Courage is much more than human capacity. No one has adequate facility to embody courage without the Spirit of Christ. It's Christ's power resting on and empowering us toward courage that honors and pleases him. Remember: when we are weak, Christ is strong. His power is made perfect in our weakness, which is the whole point of this book. His grace will always be sufficient to fuel our heart toward righteousness and kingdom living.

Therefore, persevering love requires courage. And a persevering love is best discovered in prayer, where we are reminded daily of God's persevering love for us. As we spend time in the Word, in prayer and in reflection, we are brought back to a place of devotion and dependency on the Lord. We recognize in that safe place of honest fellowship how many times God has persevered on our behalf, tolerating our inconsistencies, idiosyncrasies and idolatries. As we've received his unfailing love and faithfulness exhibited toward us, so too are we emboldened to share this with others. God's love never fails; his arms are always wide open.

I listened to a friend share from the depth of his heart his renewed insight about a troubled loved one. "She's making choices few are pleased with. She's living a lifestyle we're all concerned about. She's walking in a direction that appears to be contrary to how she was raised. Many have expressed my deepest convictions. We've done what we can to convince her otherwise. We've not succeeded; she's determined to move forward. So we have a choice. Will we love her unconditionally and stand with her in these decisions? Will we speak the truth in love? Or will we walk away angry, disappointed, disheartened? Will we choose to love her in spite of and regardless of, or will we close the door and keep her out?"

He continues, "These are some of our toughest days as family. We want the very best for all of our loved ones. Always. And everywhere I turn in ministry I hear similar stories of angst and confusion. What is the best approach? We all want to know. But in our fellowship we've all come from families of origin that differed in their approach—some from very conditional backgrounds, others were much more unconditional. What will we choose for ourselves? How will we lead our own generation toward God and his loving, unrestricted, unreserved, unmerited mercy and grace? With expectations of obedience as we define it, or with love that will never end no matter the final result?" I thought to myself, *Wow, Lord, you are certainly pursuing my brother, his family and his congregation and putting their courage to the test.*

With outstretched arms of love his family determines to be compelled to love their loved one no matter what. He concludes, "We need to be done with the anger and judgmental attitude. We need to be through with trying to convince or cajole her to make choices that simply please us. We need to be finished with seeking our own way and not submitting to God's way or even her way. We need to release our opinions, all the while making sure she knows how we feel, but we're not stopping our love. We want a relationship with her no matter what choices she makes. We're compelled to love her and delighted to do so. She's our loved one. She's the apple of our eyes. She's a dearly loved child. She's always on our heart and mind. She's deserving of our love simply because. Lord, without you we can do none of this." I'm awestruck by their deep love.

I imagine what the church of Jesus Christ would look like if we all were constrained by love, no matter what. I dream about the day when the church will live like Jesus, with outstretched arms of love. I envision the time when we walk into our local church sanctuary and see a crucifix on one side of the church and an empty cross on the other—remembering both his sacrifice and suffering, as well as his redemption and resurrection. I salivate over the notion that someday the church will actually demonstrate love, first and foremost to God, then to one another, and then outwardly to the world, always with open, outstretched arms of love. If we were ever to do so, we'd never have conflict or strife or division but instead unity, community and joy like never before. Imagine if the world actually saw us guard each other's dignity and knew with certainty that we were Christians by our love. Imagine if we really believed that God is love and that without love we are nothing, if we actually voiced and showed expressions of love to God and one another that were invitational and relational, truly sacrificial and experiential. The church and the world would look much different from how we look today. The church would make Jesus smile.

Yes, let's imagine living with outstretched arms of love. Better yet, let's choose to live with unqualified, unsurpassed, unparalleled, unconditional, over-the-top prodigal love for God and one another. Our lives will never be the same. Jesus will smile.

The Scriptures admonish us to hear and receive the central message of God's never-ending, eternal love for us. We know with certainty that he wanted us, "For he chose us in him before the creation of the world to be holy and blameless in his sight. In love he predestined us to be adopted . . . through Jesus Christ, in accordance with his pleasure and will" (Ephesians 1:4-5). He died for us: "God demonstrates his own love for us in this: While we were still sinners, Christ died for us" (Romans 5:8). He will never leave us: "Never will I leave you; never will I forsake you" (Hebrews 13:5). In fact, the amazing truth is that nothing at all can separate us from God's eternal love: "I am convinced that neither death nor life, neither angels nor demons, neither the present nor the future, nor any powers, neither height nor depth, nor anything else in all creation, will be able to separate us from the love of God that is in Christ Jesus our Lord" (Romans 8:38-39). The Greek word translated "fails" in the NIV is actually related to a verb meaning "to fall." The idea is that God's love will not fall or falter; it is constant and forever. As God says through the words of the prophet Jeremiah, "I have loved you with an everlasting love; I have drawn you with loving-kindness" (Jeremiah 31:3). What, therefore, will be your response?

If we are ever to live with outstretched arms of love, we must first repent of our failure to do so many times over. This has been the way of the past, it's certainly our present experience, and undoubtedly we'll need to repent in the future. We've all had opportunities to love without fail, and we've blown it countless times. Is this your moment to confess such blatant errors, turn away from such attitudes and actions, and consider a new way of living more redemptively?

True transformation comes from embracing our failures and then welcoming God's work of redemption. Moving from failure to triumph, from quitting to victory, from incomplete to perfect love, begins with repentance. This is the only way to experience the fullness of the resurrection life. Paul reminds the Corinthians of this by devoting the entirety of chapter 15 of his first letter to the topic of resurrection—of Christ, of the dead and of our own body. "Listen, I tell you a mystery: We will not all sleep, but we will all be changed—in a flash, in the twinkling of an eye, at the last trumpet. . . . Therefore, . . . stand firm. Let nothing move you. Always give yourselves fully to the work of the Lord, because you know that your labor in the Lord is not in vain" (1 Corinthians 15:51, 58). He preached his invitation confidently because of the reality of the resurrection life. Since love never ends, his simple mandate is issued over and over again: come close, draw near and choose to live abundantly in Christ, the one in whom love never ends, fails or dies.

Love never ends—it lasts eternally, to the very end and beyond. Love never dies. How does this form and fashion your pursuit of godliness and your leadership of others? Is your message one of eternal significance and focus, or is it altered and undermined by the pressures of this world and the compulsions of the here and now?

Love never quits—it never stops being love. God's love is not only eternal but also redemptive. Jesus offers us redemptive love that turns our repentance upside down and releases from within us a joy that knows no end. All of this is possible by the gift of his forgiving love. Will this be your platform for ministry and your posture toward all who cross your path?

Love never fades—it always is a bright beacon of light. Other gifts will fade away, but love shines brightly to the end and beyond. When we focus the spotlight too much on the earthly minded worldliness that barrages and plagues our minds, we lose sight of the light of Christ. How will the bright light of Christ's unfading love enlighten you and yours? How will the light of Christ diminish all the compulsions that seek to dominate your heart?

Love never fails—it is never outdone by any other gift or source. Love supersedes all other virtues and outlasts them to the end. Nothing we do can change the fact that God's love will always be in pursuit of our heart. Our human ability to love will fail and end (at times and at the end times) but not God's everlasting and eternal love. In the midst of your own failures, how will you release your brokenness into the loving hand of God?

There is nothing impulsive about God's love. It is not based on whims, feelings or passing fancies. His love is rock-solid, intent on benefitting the one loved, regardless of the cost. God's love perseveres, never fails and never ends. So shall it be for our love in return. When we lead our own lives and serve all who follow us, the unfailing love of God will outshine every diminution of his holy love that we seek to offer in his name. Love never ends or fails. You can hang your hat on that truth forever.

Spiritual Leadership Audit

Restoring God's Unfailing Love

There is supernatural power in the words "'My grace is sufficient for you, for my power is made perfect in your weakness.' Therefore I will boast all the more gladly about my weaknesses, so that Christ's power may rest on me. That is why, for Christ's sake, I delight in weaknesses, in insults, in hardships, in persecutions, in difficulties. For when I am weak, then I am strong" (2 Corinthians 12:9-10). As you consider your desire to lead with a courageous and persevering love—for God, self and others—it's important to reflect prayerfully on the truth that it's impossible to do so without Christ. The Spirit of Christ is our only hope for perseverance in this life.

When we consider the truth that love never ends, quits, fails or fades, we think solely of God, the one who perfected the art of loving. Our love for self and others regularly ends, quits, fails and fades. Our sinfulness and pride stand in the way of loving so completely and continuously. We all need the grace and mercy of God, without which our suffering will never be fully redeemed and our sacrifice will never bring forth the kind of renewal we long for.

Our love for God, self and others will never look like what Paul describes without allowing God to infuse our hearts with his love. All other forms are incomplete and lacking the incredible power of the love of God. Trust today that God desires and delights to fill you up with his love so that your life is changed from the inside out and your service to others births abundant life in Christ.

Confess your brokenness: Naming your brokenness and owning it as a present reality.

- In what way(s) have you found yourself failing to love God, self or others most recently? Or how have you failed to fully receive

God's unfailing love or been fearful to experience love from another?

- Consider prayerfully the details of this experience and recount them here.

Rest and trust in God's abiding presence and peace: Seeking God's unfailing love to be revealed and released from within your soul.

- *Hopeful in Scripture*: Read Romans 8:38-39 and write out Paul's words of conviction that we will not be separated from the love of God in Christ Jesus our Lord.

- *Faithful in prayer*: How will you embrace in your heart the unfailing love of God for you, which applies to every aspect of your life and leadership today?

- *Thankful in reflection*: Who in your sphere of influence needs to know both God's and your unfailing, unconditional love? How will you be a reminder of a love that perseveres and never fails toward that person?

Invite God to redeem your brokenness: Restoring God's loving perseverance and unfailing love in you. It takes Holy Spirit–empowered courage and tenacity to persevere in love and produce forbearance in our heart.

- Authenticity is the place of genuine confession about the true feelings, fears and frustrations that hinder our courage to persevere in true love from God. What do you need to confess today?

- Attentiveness is the manner in which we sharpen our vision for God, our ability to hear his voice and our longing to live obediently. What is the desire of your heart today for receiving more of God's unfailing love?

- Awareness is the ongoing discipline of noticing God and then responding with faith, hope and love. What longings for God and his unfailing love are growing in your heart today?

- Awe is the worshipful response to the many initiatives God delivers to you on a daily, moment-by-moment basis. What is your prayerful and joyful reaction to the steadfast love of God?

thirteen

Befriending Brokenness and Inviting Redemption

The greatest of these is love

WHEN THE APOSTLE PAUL CONFRONTED the Corinthian believers, the church in that secular city had begun to deteriorate ethically on the inside and became tattered morally at the outer edges. The infidelity and immorality of Corinth was well known, and the church had suffered as a result. The word *Corinthian* itself was synonymous with the term *hell-raiser* and to "Corinthianize" meant to engage in lascivious acts such as prostitution. Affluence and immorality were hallmarks of the city at the time of Paul. The cultural worship of the goddess Aphrodite complicated the setting even more. There was a magnificent temple dedicated to this goddess in Corinth. There were also other temples to other gods and a pantheon to all gods. The city was home to other cult worship and in essence became a place where anything goes, even in its theology. So Paul writes from Ephesus to the believers in Corinth, answering some of their questions as well as speaking truth into concerns he had for the church.

As we have discovered together throughout this book, the issues Paul addresses in these letters are filled with spiritual, ethical and moral implications. The disorders and faults addressed in his first letter are varied and many: divisive factions, rampant immorality and ongoing litigation among members. Plus he tackles the behavior of women in worship, abuses of the Lord's Table, questions about spiritual gifts, doctrinal errors and even procedures for disbursing their offerings. Additionally, he replies to questions about marriage, separation, reconciliation and celibacy.

In 2 Corinthians, he defends his ministry and teaches them the priorities of ministry relationally, practically and theologically. Issues of relationships, transparency, wealth, reputation, accountability, reconciliation and outreach are the order of the day in this letter.

Both letters are filled with incredible depth of wisdom, directed to the church and inspired by the Holy Spirit in very specific ways. "Follow the way of love" (1 Corinthians 14:1), therefore, is a good summary statement for all of Paul's instructions. For though faith, hope and love will all remain a part of the community of faith into eternity, the greatest is love. *Faith* will last forever as we put our wholehearted trust in Christ for all eternity. *Hope* will also remain as the promise of eternal life keeps it alive and keeps the future bright with the promises of God to refresh and renew his people forever. Yet the most excellent way to live and serve is *love*, which will outshine and outlast and outweigh the others in importance.

Written to remind this dysfunctional church not to overrate gifts, compete with each other and abuse the spiritual gifts, 1 Corinthians 13 is a sharp rebuke to a church gone awry from God's priorities. Although read most often at wedding ceremonies today, it was not, as we've already mentioned, written for this purpose (while it still applies nicely and is very appropriate when consecrating a new household of faith in the holy bonds of matrimony). *Love* here is an action verb, one that emanates in the heart's attitude and is realized in behavior. It is not meant to be a schmaltzy sentimentality.

There is a sweeping contrast in the text between what will not last forever—prophecies, tongues and knowledge—with that which will last forever: faith, hope and love. The former three gifts will eventually fade away in this life, but the latter three attributes will abide forever. Faith will breed hope, and both will abide because of love. Love is the greatest axiom for sustaining life in all its fullness as it affects everything we are, have and do. Love lasts forever and surpasses all other aspects of our lives bar none.

God is love. For God to love he doesn't just speak love or do love; he *is* love. Not *eros* (romance) or *phileo* (brotherly love) or *storge* (family affection), but *agape*—unconditional love. To know *agape* one must first know God, the author and sole supplier of unconditional love. To know God is to know this kind of love.

In order to offer such love, we must first receive it for ourselves. Paul wanted that for the Corinthians more than anything else. The need is the same today: there is nothing more important than love. But we often live without full recognition of the unconditional, generous, grace-filled, lavishing, over-the-top, affectionate, warm, intimate, magnificent, glorious, heartfelt, wonderful, amazing, joy-filled, inconceivable, eternal (add your own descriptors) *love of God*. Instead, we live, work, serve and give as hard and as much and as long as possible without the Spirit's loving wind in our sail to keep us afloat and moving forward with supernatural power.

Leaders without the empowerment of God's eternal love will undoubtedly let other priorities take over the first place God so desires. Even such beauties as the spiritual gifts, which reflect the empowering presence of the Holy Spirit, as well as faith and hope—all will remain subservient to the priority of love. If it sounds too mushy, read the biblical text without the focus on love, and it won't have much substance at all. Love is the reason, the essence, the focus, the central priority of the Christian and all faith communities of all time. Let love reign in your heart and life and watch how your world is transformed right before your eyes. For Paul, there was no other way; he wanted his followers to know and live likewise. The greatest of all is love.

INVITATION TO REORDER LOVES

The brilliant American theologian Jonathan Edwards (1703–1758) wrote prolifically about the importance of religious affections. Centuries prior to Edwards, the religious genius Saint Augustine (354–430) gave voice to the significance of reordering our loves. Since then, great authors such as C. S. Lewis, who wrote about the four loves and how to maintain an active presence in loving others, as well as the late social activist Dorothy Day have written about the priority of love. Each encouraged a revolution of the heart and has stirred us to consider the invitation that Jesus, Paul, John, the prophets, psalmists and other biblical writers originally asked when considering love as the greatest urgency of all. There simply isn't a better way to live than to love—and to always love with the entirety of our heart, soul, mind and strength, with God as our number one priority.

In one of the more remarkable post-resurrection settings, written about in John 21:1-14, the disciples, who had been fishing in the Sea of Tiberias, find Jesus along the seashore cooking breakfast for them. Seeing that they had found little success, Jesus calls out to them with some advice: "Throw the net on the right side of the boat and you will find some [fish]." When they did so, they were unable to haul the net in because of the large number of fish (153 to be exact). After a hearty meal of fish and bread, Jesus asks Peter, "Do you truly love me more than these?" (John 21:15).

In that moment he is asking Peter about his affections. The question could have meant, "Do you love me more than these other disciples love me?" Or it could have been more like, "Do you love me more than you love these other disciples?" Or a third option: "Do you love me more than you love these things (your fishing nets and equipment or the fish you just caught and the profit they represent)?" Regardless of the true meaning of the question (which scholars have yet to agree on), each one is worth our consideration. Is love for Jesus something we measure competitively against others' affection for Jesus? Or is it comparative to others we love? Or is our love for Jesus contrasted with our affection(s) for other things, as in our possessions and portfolios?

Peter's answer says it all, "Yes, Lord, you know that I love you" (John 21:15). But Jesus asks the same question two more times. Most biblical scholars would agree that this is because Peter denied him three times just prior to his crucifixion, and his reinstatement is three questions affirming his affection for Jesus. Regardless, the test is the same: *Do you love me more than these?* The end result is the reordering of affection: yes, Lord, you know that I love you.

That same question comes to us as leaders and followers today. Each and every day we are consciously or unconsciously confronted with the simple inquiry, "Do you love Jesus more than these?" Therefore we must consider prayerfully our answer before too glibly offering a response. It's far too easy to repeat Peter's words, "Yes, Lord, you know that I love you" when in fact we have wandered far from our love for Jesus and have chosen other affections instead of or more than him.

If the soul is the most neglected part of the person, then God is the most neglected love of the person. It's time that we come clean with our true affections, the ones that occupy and preoccupy our hearts and minds on a daily basis. These are the loves that need to be reordered. Some need to be eliminated altogether due to their inappropriateness, and others simply need to get prioritized or reprioritized more accurately. To love our family, our friends, even ourselves is not bad whatsoever, but when these loves are greater and stronger than our love for God, they need to be placed in their proper sequence. Otherwise our hearts will continue to lean away from God and instead find strength in various other segments of life.

There are so many other affections tugging at the soul today. Our *enemy the devil* is the first one to pull us off course and into his schemes of trickery, mockery and malicious intent. The enemy of our souls convinces us to live prideful existences as if we're our own sovereign nation, without any need for another. There are *idols of our heart* that breed contempt in our soul and cajole us to feed them regularly, such as the alluring triumvirate of money, sex and power. The Internet and *all forms of technology* keep us focused on the addiction of information, skimming the surface of any number of preoccupations. *Busyness* is another soul killer, as is her evil stepsister, *Sabbath neglect.* All of these options that destroy our focus on the priority of love for Jesus need to be identified, called out by name, and labeled as "idol" or "evil" or named more specifically within the broader categories of money, sex or power.

After the idols of our heart have been identified comes the *reordering of our affections*. Note the ones that need to be eliminated as well as the ones that need to be reordered. List them in writing. Pray over them. Ask the Spirit to do his work of relinquishment in your heart. Invite the Spirit of God to give you the strength and perseverance you will need to do the hard work necessary in reordering your loves.

Once we've reordered our affections and relinquished our idols, it's time to restore our priorities so that we can remain refreshed and renewed in body, mind, heart and soul. Slowing down long enough to enter Sabbath rest is the starting point. We need time to pause, ponder and pray with the living God to address and re-address the most fundamental question, "Do you love me more than these?" Putting God back in the front of the line, making him the number one priority of our heart and soul and keeping him in his rightfully sovereign place in our life is a daily, sometimes hourly, choice of the will. But, you will never fully identify the contents of your racing heart and mind without first pressing the pause button of your full to overflowing life. Stop. Notice. Listen. Pray. Reorder. Live. Serve. Repeat.

Unless the rhythms and relationships that define our life are considered and reconsidered, we may never understand the importance of reordering our loves. Without some kind of regular activities that ooze accountability and honest reflection, we may live a full and active life, but it may in fact become quite boring and unfulfilling over time. The beauty of Sabbath rest is that it brings us back to the reality that only God is God; we are not God, and we desperately need God.

God rested after his work and so must we. Honoring of Sabbath holiness is one of his Ten Commandments, and we must comply. He prioritized and personalized Sabbath when his Son Jesus walked among us and was often found in a set apart place to pray, as we must do. And he's prepared for us an eternal resting place in heaven and wants us to practice Sabbath rest while here on earth. Without such rest we will not experience true renewal for our weary soul.

Life and love are intimately intertwined. Without love there is no life, and without life there is no love. How we love affects how we live, and how we live affects how we love. Therefore, keeping both in check is one of the most important issues affecting the vitality of the soul. What is your choice today?

THE GREATEST OF ALL—FAITH, HOPE AND LOVE—IS LOVE

Kintsugi is a Japanese form of art where broken pottery is mended with lines of gold filigree. For those who practice this unique art form, the beauty is discovered in the brokenness of the pottery. Without the brokenness, the artist would not be able to rebuild the stoneware into its original design. Mending the broken pot requires skillful, patient and loving hands. Best of all, the gold strengthens the weakness, and the end result is better than new. In fact, it's the brokenness that creates the ultimate strength and beauty of the pot.

So it is with Christ's gospel of love. Created and loved into being ourselves, we are eventually and quite frequently broken due to internal or external forces that corrupt our original design. Without Christ's redeeming love putting our lives back together over and over again, we remain in that state of brokenness. But when we receive his loving embrace and welcome his restorative hands of grace, he re-creatively puts us back together again one piece at a time. We are not fully restored this side of heaven, for we await his return when our full redemption occurs. In the meantime, we welcome his work of sanctification, and it is here where our beauty as created and loved beings is re-formed in Christ. It is the golden strand of Christ's restorative and redemptive love that holds us together, stronger than ever before. This is the only way to be *broken and whole*.

Imagine once again what your life would look like if you saw your redeemed and restored brokenness as producing strength rather than simply as a weakness to tolerate. Imagine if you were to consider Christ's transformation of your broken parts as the filigree that makes for a fuller, richer, redemptive and more beautiful life. Imagine if your life were strengthened with strands of gold that held all the restored broken parts back in their rightful place, and beauty re-emerged from the inside out, through every crevice of your heart and life.

This is so counter to the ways we've been taught to mend a broken life today. The methods of our world look more like hard work heaped upon more hard work, and if that's not enough, then add a dose of shame, ridicule, comparison, finger pointing and judgment to top it off. Even well-meaning Christian leaders are found in such postures toward those who are different from them, who look at life through other lenses, or who come to different conclusions about how we're "all" to live our lives. The Christian life is continually defined by what we should and should not do, say or think. We've so divided ourselves into quadrants and categories that we almost can't help but be dogmatic, opinionated and harshly judgmental. As a result, we tend to look at those closest to us in such a manner. We make statements about how others should be living differently all the while ignoring the plank in our own eyes. Didn't Jesus have something to say about this? As leaders, we've become judgmental; the twinkle in our eyes has been lost and replaced instead by a scowl and a frown. Is that what's become of your picture of God and your preferred reflection too? Imagine if that were replaced with a wink of affection instead.

Many believers struggle with brokenness and see their brokenness as something to conquer—yes, with some prayer, but more with sheer willpower. Who takes the time to pause, ponder and receive the redemptive love of God more fully? Some look at their brokenness and strive to "fix" it by "pulling themselves up by the boot straps" or hunkering down and finally getting serious about it or working harder in order to overcome their annoying issues, rather than seeing their brokenness as windows into their soul, or even as opportunities to experience redemption and transformation—something to embrace rather than tackle, as if we can overcome brokenness by our own strength.

When leaders and followers can discover and embrace—even befriend—our core area(s) of brokenness, it becomes an entree into freedom as we release it into the gracious hands of God. If we are able to form an inner sanctuary of grace, being held affectionately by God who restores our suffering with his loving embrace, we can indeed understand the power of redemptive, restorative love offered to us by an unconditionally loving and grace-filled God. God's love is the greatest healer, the golden filigree of restoration and redemption of every ounce of pain being carried by the overburdened life. Responding affirmatively to God's invitation to receive such love ushers us into a healing that's transformational for ourselves and all who cross our path.

My firm belief is that for the average and, yes, broken (as we all are) leader today seeking a more intimate walk with God as the "restoration and renewal expert" for our soul, there is indeed hope and joy in the process of whole-life transformation. God is Redeemer—his longing is to renew and transform us from the inside out. As the great shepherd of our souls, even in the presence of my (internal and external) enemies, "he restores my soul" (Psalm 23:3). God delights in the ongoing process of shepherding my soul and loving me back to redemptive wholeness and grace-filled living, all through an extension of his steadfast love and mercy.

This is the posture of leadership needed today: a leader who recognizes life as abundantly rich and beautifully designed, held together by the golden strands of loving grace and forgiving mercy, where both strengths and brokenness are continuously released, redeemed, restored and renewed for God's glory. This message must first be graciously received and then generously offered to others in Jesus' name. We are free in Christ to be both broken and whole—and on the pathway to spiritual transformation all the days of our lives.

By forming an inner sanctuary of grace, we will begin to see with fresh, new eyes the power of redemptive love. In such a place, we are delightfully held in God's loving and eternal embrace. May it be so. All for the glory of God and his everlasting kingdom of grace.

Spiritual Leadership Audit

Reordering Your Loves

We have been shown the most excellent way. With these three remaining—faith, hope and love—the greatest of these is always love. So, do you love Jesus more than any or all of your particular versions of the "these" that captivate your heart? As you read and reflect on all that's been written, your first response may be confession. To embrace with honesty and vulnerability your brokenness that keeps your affection for Christ much lower on the priority list than it should be might lead to an admission of pride or guilt. If so, it's time to come home to Jesus and release that into his loving hands. Come clean of your sinful patterns of distraction from and distortion of God's love, and ask the Lord to forgive, restore and renew you once more.

If you've been working so hard that you've ignored Sabbath as a day and a lifestyle, then it may be time to make some hard decisions and relinquish control of your life and schedule to God. If money, sex or power have gone to your head and selfishly affected your decision making, leadership and lifestyle, then it's time to come home to the affectionate arms of God where such distractions can be relinquished.

Be honest. Come clean. Confess sin. Embrace brokenness. Seek restoration. Experience abundant life once more. *Join the fellowship of the broken and whole.* Walk the path to spiritual transformation today and always. Let love be your guide. Amen.

Confess your brokenness: Naming your brokenness and owning it as a present reality.

- In what way(s) have you found yourself with disordered loves, or have you experienced disordered loves from or in another, most recently?

- Consider prayerfully the details of this experience and recount them here.

Rest and trust in God's abiding presence and peace: Seeking God's reordered affection to be revealed and released from within your soul.

- *Hopeful in Scripture*: Enter the scene at the breakfast bonfire with Jesus and the other disciples in John 21. Read the account with eagerness and anticipation, placing yourself in Peter's position, being asked by Jesus, "Do you love me more than these?" What is your reply?

- *Faithful in prayer*: Sit with the question, "What or who do you love more than Jesus?"

- *Thankful in reflection*: When is the last time you simply gave up what normally would be a productive hour and turned it upside down into an hour of life-giving rest for your soul? What were the necessary components, and how can you make more of a habit of this in the future?

Invite God to redeem your brokenness: Restoring God's loving priority in you. The reordering of your loves will take a lifetime to accomplish. It's only possible as you submit to the loving will of God, entrust your heart into the Father's faithful hands and remain empowered by the Spirit of God, so that you may live and love as Jesus invites you as his beloved disciple. This will require the dismantling of affections that have become idols in your heart. Money, sex and power are three dominant themes to consider. Reflect on the following questions.

- Reorder your affection for people: Who in your life has an unhealthy grip on your heart today? Open your hands and release them into God's tender, loving care.

- Reorder your affection for possessions: What do you own that you instead need to steward and possibly give away? Consider being extravagantly generous with what you possess.

- Reorder your affection for power: What areas of life do you dominate (needing to win the race, conquer the prize, control the outcome, manipulate others, carry convictions and hold fast to attitudes) in order to be in control? Prayerfully invite others to speak into your propensity to always need to win.

- Reorder your affection for persuasions: How has the enemy of your soul tantalized you with enticements? Or how have your addictions consumed you or technology supplanted soul and self-care? How have such persuasions led you outside the will of God? Confess the temptations you have succumbed to and be set free.

- Reorder your priorities and make space for Sabbath rest. What needs to be released in your life so that you can truly "slow down and be more"? Consider Sabbath practices that create life-transforming space for God to remain number one in your heart and life.

Conclusion and Benediction

Broken and Whole

THANKS FOR JOINING ME on a journey toward spiritual wholeness, the discovery of God's incredible strength in the context
of our unique set of weaknesses. Are you beginning to see the
value of embracing your brokenness, submitting it into God's
gracious hands and finding hope for how he will restore, redeem
and renew it all for his glory?

Congratulations for courageously reviewing and then prayerfully and intentionally considering your areas of brokenness and
weakness, as well as the infliction of others' brokenness upon
you. This book was not intended to be a definitive work on the
subject of brokenness but, hopefully, one that illuminates some
of the most common ways brokenness and weakness affect the
life of a follower of Christ and especially a leader in the body of
Christ. We've covered the waterfront for sure: impatience,
mean-spiritedness, envy, jealousy, competition, pride, abuse,
rudeness, self-centeredness, anger, evil intent, lies, cowardice,
failures and addictions, just to name a few. All of these hinder
our fellowship with God and undermine our relationships and

leadership. I'm profoundly grateful for your willingness to contemplate the many ways the flip side of love is experienced in
your brokenness.

But thanks be to God, our brokenness and weakness can be
redeemed for his glory—if we are open and receptive to his life-
transforming love. We've taken time to prayerfully consider the
sixteen words and phrases that define God's love as he so desires
for it to be lived out in us:

1. Love is patient.

2. Love is kind.

3. Love does not envy.

4. Love does not boast.

5. Love is not proud.

6. Love is not rude.

7. Love is not self-seeking.

8. Love is not easily angered.

9. Love keeps no record of wrongs.

10. Love does not delight in evil.

11. Love rejoices in the truth.

12. Love always protects.

13. Love always trusts.

14. Love always hopes.

15. Love always perseveres.

16. Love never fails.

> And now these
> three remain:
> faith, hope
> and love.
> But the greatest
> of these is love.
> (1 Corinthians 13:13)

We've paused and considered the meaning of each of these
words and phrases for the sake of our soul and the depth of our
relationships with God, others and ourselves. We've unlocked

the keys to the most excellent way of living, loving and leading. I hope you have engaged in the audits at the end of each chapter, designed for deep soul reflection and renewal. You may want to walk through your responses with your team or a spiritual companion and continue to pray into each of the areas that seemed most relevant for you in this season of your life and leadership.

You also might want to consider how this foundation of love affects your rule of life. If so, take a look at my book *Crafting a Rule of Life.* Visit the website created for those who are currently working on theirs too: ruleoflife.com. Your rule of life will help you frame your understanding of God's call on your life: your roles, gifts, passion, vision and mission, and how this is being lived out in your spiritual, relational, physical, financial and missional priorities. It will help you define all of this in your daily, weekly, monthly, quarterly and annual rhythms. Most important, it's a helpful, practical, life-giving process worthy of your pursuit, especially now that you've concluded the book in your hands.

Bottom line from my heart to yours: discovering the true you as you grow in knowing and experiencing the true God will deeply influence your way forward in all areas of life. Beginning each day acknowledging your need for God because of your weakness and propensity to try and "be god" will lead you into a deeper trust in and love for God. Your life with God will be all the richer. May it be so for you and those you serve!

Receive now the benediction I've written with you in mind, my comrade on this journey toward wholeness as a broken, beloved and blessed leader in the body of Christ.

The Benediction

For all leaders who are broken and whole
on the pathway to spiritual transformation:
Remember the gospel of unconditional love,
and be captivated by Christ.
Receive God's joyful gifts of faith, hope and love.
Our Father holds you gently in love's sanctifying
and transforming embrace.
The Lord Jesus Christ desires to gracefully
forgive and redeem your brokenness.
As the Spirit does his renewing work in your heart
and life, strength will emerge from weakness.
When you serve others, offer hope for reconciliation
and restoration in the kingdom of God.
Live, love and lead in the name of God;
Father, Son and Holy Spirit. Amen.

Acknowledgments

ALL WRITING PROJECTS ARE A TEAM EFFORT. I'm profoundly grateful to God for all who poured courage into my heart for the completion of this book. I could not have written *Broken and Whole* were it not for those who came alongside me with affirming words, prayerful hearts, listening ears and lots of wise counsel.

First, special thanks to Cindy Bunch, my tireless editor, and Allison Rieck, who urged me on toward a continually improved manuscript every step of the way. Thanks to Jeff Crosby and his marketing team who will help get this book into as many hands as possible. IVP, you are a fabulous publishing partner, and I'm indebted to your belief in my vision for this important message to be conveyed to spiritual leaders everywhere.

Second, I'm grateful to the teams I'm privileged to serve who make my life and ministry so delightful. Thank you, Leadership Transformations (LTI) Board of Directors and Inner Circle for your steadfast love and prayerful support. Thank you to the entire LTI Ministry Team for your faithful partnership in service to thousands of leaders each year. Thank you, fabulous Pierce Center team, as well as all the Pierce Fellows and alumni and our Spiritual Formation Doctor of Ministry cohorts at Gordon-Conwell Theological Seminary. Each team brings me more joy than words can adequately express.

Third, to my life-shaping circle of friends (too numerous to mention all of you by name), my life-transforming community of faith at SSJE, and my life-giving, tested-and-true family, especially Bekah, Nate and Ashley: thank you one and all from the bottom of my heart. I'm grateful for your abiding love that upholds this broken and whole leader. You are loved more than you'll ever fully comprehend this side of heaven.

Most of all, to Ruthie, none of this work is ever a meaningful reality without your love, grace, patience and joy. I'm speechless and forever grateful for your partnership in life and ministry.

This writing project has been a labor of love for the body of Christ and all who are called to serve the church. To God alone belongs all the glory, honor and praise.

About the Author

Stephen A. Macchia (MDiv, DMin) is the founder and president of Leadership Transformations, Inc., a spiritual formation ministry founded in 2003 and focused on leaders and teams in local church and parachurch ministry settings nationwide (leadershiptransformations.org). He is also the director of the Pierce Center for Disciple-Building and teaches in the Doctor of Ministry Spiritual Formation for Ministry Leaders track at Gordon-Conwell Theological Seminary. He previously served as president of Vision New England (1989–2003), a ministry devoted to creating a large network of services for and among six thousand congregations from eighty different denominations in the six-state region. Prior to that he was on the pastoral staff team at Grace Chapel in Lexington, Massachusetts, (1978–1989) in four pastoral roles including senior associate pastor.

Steve is the author of several books including *Becoming a Healthy Church* (Baker), *Becoming a Healthy Church Workbook* (Baker), *Becoming a Healthy Disciple* (Baker/LTI), *Becoming a Healthy Disciple Small Group Study and Worship Guide* (LTI), *Becoming a Healthy Team* (Baker/LTI), *Becoming a Healthy Team Exercises* (LTI), *Crafting a Rule of Life* (ruleoflife.com; InterVarsity Press), *Path of a Beloved Disciple: 31 Days in the Gospel of John* (LTI), *Wellspring: 31 Days to Whole-Hearted Living* (LTI) and most recently *Outstretched Arms of Grace: A 40-Day Lenten Devotional* (LTI). Some of Steve's books are translated into Korean, Spanish, Chinese, Russian and Thai. Steve and his wife, Ruth, have two grown children, Nathan and Rebekah, and live in greater Boston.

LEADERSHIP
TRANSFORMATIONS <small>INC.</small>

FORMATION | DISCERNMENT | RENEWAL

Our vision: For local churches and Christian organizations to be filled with leaders who place spiritual formation, discernment and renewal above all other leadership priorities.

Our mission: To cultivate vibrant spirituality and attentive discernment among Christian leaders and teams.

Our ministries:

- Emmaus: Spiritual Leadership Communities
- Selah: spiritual direction certificate program
- Soul care retreats and Soul Sabbaths
- Spiritual formation groups
- Spiritual health assessments
- Spiritual discernment for teams
- Sabbatical planning
- Spiritual formation resources

Resources available at spiritualformationstore.com:

- Ready-to-use retreat guides
- Reflective readings
- *Silencio*: free monthly resource
- Books written by Steve Macchia and the Leadership Transformations team
- Spiritual Formation Store: twenty-five categories of recommended books
- Church Health Assessment Tool (CHAT): a holistic, biblical church health survey (healthychurch.net)

Visit www.leadershiptransformations.org
Or call toll free (877) TEAM-LTI

Also by Stephen A. Macchia

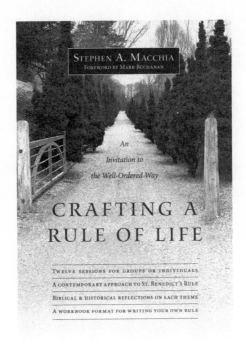

Crafting a Rule of Life: An Invitation to the Well-Ordered Way
978-0-8308-3564-5

formatio
TRADITION. EXPERIENCE.
TRANSFORMATION.

Formatio books from InterVarsity Press follow the rich tradition of the church in the journey of spiritual formation. These books are not merely about being informed, but about being transformed by Christ and conformed to his image. Formatio stands in InterVarsity Press's evangelical publishing tradition by integrating God's Word with spiritual practice and by prompting readers to move from inward change to outward witness. InterVarsity Press uses the chambered nautilus for Formatio, a symbol of spiritual formation because of its continual spiral journey outward as it moves from its center. We believe that each of us is made with a deep desire to be in God's presence. Formatio books help us to fulfill our deepest desires and to become our true selves in light of God's grace.